MAKING VOTES COUNT

Martin Linton has been Labour MP for Battersea since 1997. Previously he was a journalist on *The Guardian*. He edited *The Guardian's Election Guide* (1997) and its *Guide to the House of Commons* (1992). He has written books and articles on the reform of the voting system, the funding of political parties and the influence of the media in elections. He is a sponsor of the Labour Campaign for Electoral Reform.

Mary Southcott researches, writes and speaks about politics, briefing politicians and the media as the Labour Campaign for Electoral Reform's parliamentary and political officer. A member of Labour's National Policy Forum and the South & West Regional Executive, she was on the Foreign & Security Policy Commission and is Secretary of the all-party Friends of Cyprus. She is a trustee of Pathway Star, which provides residential rehabilitation from addiction for women.

MAKING VOTES COUNT

THE CASE FOR ELECTORAL REFORM

by

Martin Linton

and

Mary Southcott

Foreword by

Robin Cook

P

PROFILE BOOKS

First published in Great Britain in 1998 by
Profile Books Ltd
62 Queen Anne Street
London W1M 9LA

Typeset in Galliard by MacGuru
macguru@pavilion.co.uk
Printed in Great Britain by Biddles Ltd

A CIP catalogue record for this book is available from the British Library.

ISBN 1 86197 087 0

CONTENTS

ACKNOWLEDGEMENTS

We are grateful to all those who have discussed these ideas with us: to Robin Cook for his introduction; to John Curtice, at the University of Strathclyde, who prepared a number of the tables and statistics for the first edition and continues to help us all understand elections and electoral reform better; and to Gordon Reece, University of Bristol, for his time and psephology, as well as for being right when his 1980s model predicted how the very nature of the Conservatives' success, their geographically spread support, left them vulnerable to being wiped out in many parts of the country if they fell below a third of the national vote. We would like to thank Jim McCormick and Deborah Pate for their ideas as much as their proofreading and also the Joseph Rowntree Reform Trust, without which much of the work for reform would never have been possible.

We dedicate this book to a new generation of voters, to Polly and Essie, Caroline and Emily, who will experience using new voting systems and may revisit this material if they need to be revised in the future; to all the Labour politicians up and down the country who have had the courage to change their minds; to Raymond Plant for his genuine determination to make honest politicians of us all; to members of the Labour Campaign for Electoral Reform and reformers in all parties and none who have worked for change; to the Labour leaders who have kept this issue on the party's and the nation's agenda, and to all those 1997 voters who managed to manoeuvre around the current voting system to give us a government which has promised that the people will decide the voting system in a referendum to be held within its lifetime.

We hope this book will help inform and excite those commenting on or campaigning for change in the voting referendum. Some people prefer word pictures and others need statistics. This book is written for both audiences. We hope you enjoy it.

Martin Linton and Mary Southcott
May 1998

FOREWORD

> *I am not prepared to put up with a system which once every generation, every 30 years, gives us an opportunity to get in with a majority the way the Conservatives do and govern in the same way. It is not we who pay the penalty, but the people we represent. When we win, let us seize the opportunity to change the electoral system so we do not have ever again to return to elective dictatorship of the kind we have experienced.*

This quotation first appeared on the front page of this book's predecessor in 1993. The Catch 22 of electoral reform was always that no party in government elected by the present system would ever question, let alone change, the system that put them in office. Yet within nine months of the election, Labour has kept its promise to hold referendums in Scotland and Wales and next year there will be elections to the Scottish Parliament, the Welsh Assembly and the European Parliament all using forms of proportional representation. In December 1997 we set up the Independent Commission on the Voting System for the House of Commons, chaired by Roy Jenkins, former Liberal Democrat Leader in the House of Lords.

This book is written from a Labour perspective by Labour Party members who have researched this field for over a decade. They quite properly concentrate on the change that has gone on in the Labour Party since 1987. This is not to undervalue the contribution of the Liberal Democrats to the democratic agenda or indeed that of other parties. It was from a recognition that a new constitution for the UK could not belong to any one party that Labour began discussions with the Liberal Democrats. This was itself a natural extension of the cross-party cooperation that took place in the Scottish Constitutional Convention.

The purpose of an electoral system is to enable the voters to choose their representative in Parliament and their government. When a system fails in these tasks, it is right to consider change. The intention of the first edition of the book was to show that the first-past-the-post system cannot fulfil these tasks. Nothing has happened in 1997 to undermine that judgement, only to make it more likely that change will happen.

There are still many people who have voted for one party all their lives but who have never been represented by the MP of their choice. Indeed one might expect a new surge of interest in electoral reform among Conservatives now that they have lost all their seats in Scotland and Wales. In the past it was hard to persuade commentators that Labour's interest in examining electoral reform was about democracy and not simply a cynical reaction to a long period in opposition. It should now be clear that Labour is committed to democratic reform of our political culture. That culture is profoundly affected by the system we choose to elect our political representatives.

Many of our European partners have electoral systems which encourage consensus on issues like health, education and the economy. Choosing a voting system is not just an academic exercise. If we want a society that operates on the basis of inclusion and cooperation, our electoral system must display the same characteristics.

The referendum which will be held following the recommendation of the Jenkins Commission will mean that everyone within and beyond political parties will have to make up their own minds about whether we change the system. Whatever the outcome, involving people in discussion of how they are governed is itself valuable. Clause 4 of Labour's own constitution talks about open democracy in which government is held to account by the people and decisions are taken as far as possible by the communities they affect. Labour was elected with an overwhelming majority but we recognise that does not give us ownership of Britain's constitution. That is why the final decision on our electoral system will be for voters themselves in a referendum.

There are still many people whose votes have little or no effect on the outcome of a general election. The choice of our electoral system has to make votes count wherever people live and produce a Parliament where the party strength better reflects the degree of support each party enjoys in the country.

The Jenkins Commission, and the referendum that will follow, give us the chance to have a modern electoral system fit for the new century; one that creates a closer relationship between the electorate and their government; and which helps give the British people ownership of their democracy every day and not just on election day.

Robin Cook
June 1998

1 THE OPPORTUNITY FOR CHANGE

Eras rarely start or end in neat round numbers. The general election of 1 May 1997 was not simply a new dawn or the final ending of a period people called Thatcher's era. It was the beginning of change in the way we are governed. It was the chance to move on from our 19th-century constitution and prepare for the 21st.

The landslide Labour victory, based as it was on the current first-past-the-post (FPTP) system, broke a string of records. Some of these records seem to compensate Labour for 18 wilderness years; some point to a pendulum which gets stuck and then moves dramatically; some suggest that electoral reform will be an unlikely priority for a party which is a huge beneficiary of the current system; and some show why the case for change is more compelling than ever.

In the 1997 general election:

- Labour got its largest ever majority in the House of Commons, 178 seats (in 1945 it was only 146), and its largest ever number of MPs, 418, the largest majority and the largest number since the national government in 1935. It made the largest number of gains, 145, since the 1945 election.
- Labour's share of the UK vote was 43.2 per cent, its largest since 1966, but less than Margaret Thatcher's in 1979. Labour won its second largest vote ever. Only in 1951 did it get more, but lost. But it received fewer votes than Margaret Thatcher in 1979 and 1987 and John Major in 1992 (the highest total number of votes ever cast for a British party).
- It was the poorest Conservative share of the vote, 30.7 per cent, since the Great Reform Act of 1832, with the fewest

MPs, 165, since 1906 when they had 156, although they made fewer losses, 171, than in 1945, 190.

♦ In the metropolitan counties and London, the Conservatives won only 17 MPs out of a possible 172. Labour won seats which it had never held, or last held in 1945 or 1966, in rural and southern areas. It was possible on 2 May 1997 to travel from Land's End to John o' Groats passing through only one Conservative seat.

♦ The nationalist parties did well, although the Scottish National Party gained only six seats for their 22.1 per cent of the Scottish vote. There were no Scottish Conservative MPs for the first time ever and no Welsh Conservative MPs for the first time since 1906.

♦ It was the first time that a third party gained more than a couple of dozen seats since 1929. The Liberal Democrats won 46. Their share of the vote actually fell from 17.8 per cent in 1992 to 16.8 per cent in 1997, a lower share than they had in 1974, 1983 or 1987, but the targeting of these votes gave them more MPs for fewer votes.

♦ More people voted for minor parties: Green Party, Referendum Party, UK Independence Party, Natural Law Party, Socialist Labour Party, Scottish Socialist Alliance, New Communist Party of Britain, British National Party, ProLife, The Third Way, Albion Party, Official Monster Raving Loony Party and New and Old Labour. Arthur Scargill, long-term supporter of electoral reform, saved his deposit of £500 but most minor party and fringe candidates lost theirs. There were 3,717 of these candidates, making an average of more than five per constituency.

♦ A record number of constituencies were affected by reviews of the boundary commissions. Only 174 of the previous 651 constituencies retained the same boundaries they had had in the 1992 general election. (Notional 1992 figures were calculated for the changed seats by Colin Rallings and Michael Thrasher of Plymouth University.)

- More women than ever before were elected: 120 (including the Speaker, Betty Boothroyd, the first woman to occupy this position), double the 1992 figure.
- Nine ethnic minority MPs were elected, the highest number ever, although still unrepresentative of the population as a whole.
- Three openly gay men were elected: the cabinet minister, Chris Smith, and two Labour electoral reformers, Ben Bradshaw (Exeter) and Stephen Twigg (Enfield Southgate). One minister, Angela Eagle, came out as a lesbian in September after the election.
- A total of 117 MPs retired, including many supporters of the FPTP voting system. Only six of the 38 retiring Labour MPs were sponsors of the Labour Campaign for Electoral Reform (LCER).
- There were nearly 200 known electoral reformers in the House of Commons: 46 Liberal Democrats, 10 Nationalists; over 120 MP sponsors of the Labour Campaign for Electoral Reform, some undeclared in the Conservative, Labour and Northern Ireland parties, and Martin Bell, who defeated Neil Hamilton in Tatton to become the first Independent to be elected since 1945.

As long as electoral reform is about good governance rather than the vested interest of parties, this new political landscape provides the opportunity for change and many of the arguments for reform. The process of making a decision about the voting system started with Labour's manifesto pledge to establish an independent commission to recommend a proportional system. The task of the independent commission, set up on 1 December 1997 and chaired by Lord Jenkins of Hillhead, is to find a British proportional system which may be used in future to elect MPs to parliament.

In the referendum that follows, there are two elements to the choice which people and political parties need to make. First, can they continue to support the present system? Second, does the system on offer address some of the criticisms made of first-past-the-post (FPTP)? In other words, is it an improvement? The debate must begin with an honest appraisal of the current system. Why do we have it? How well or badly does it work? Should we change it? The following six chapters (2–8) take a long hard look at the FPTP system.

Those who now argue for change need to know that this is not the first time that attempts have been made to change the voting system for the House of Commons. The Labour Party was committed to reform in the first quarter of this century. Chapters 9–12 give a brief history of the voting system and electoral reform, particularly its recent progress inside the Labour Party.

Chapter 13 outlines the principles which lie behind a choice of system and suggests a British proportional system which electoral reformers can campaign for and which addresses some of the illogicalities of the present system. And finally, in Chapter 14, the referendum on the voting system is placed in the context of creating a more democratic politics.

The debate about the voting system generates strong emotions. That is because it is about power, who has it and how it is shared. Different voting systems give different answers. Just as in the boundary commission inquiries vested party interest lies just below the surface, so arguments of winning and losing hover over any such debate.

But what is new is the opportunity for us all to see this issue from an entirely new perspective: Labour can see it through the prism of success, the Conservatives from the perspective of failure and the Liberal Democrats, who have for years espoused the principle, can at last do more than dream about a more democratic system. They can help to create it.

WHAT'S WRONG WITH
FIRST-PAST-THE-POST?

2 **DISTORTION**

The only situation where the FPTP system works well is where there are only two candidates. The reasons should be obvious. It does not take children in a playground long to discover that you cannot toss a coin between three. As soon as you introduce third candidates into FPTP elections you introduce distortion. Third candidates, even if they have no chance of winning, will affect the chances of the other candidates and will introduce an element of irrationality into the contest.

The most obvious is the problem known as "splitting the vote". For instance, if a party of the far left decides to intervene in an election, then even if a majority supports the left, the right may win, as in Example 1, Table 2.1.

TABLE 2.1 **EXAMPLE 1**

Election 1		*Election 2*	
Left	10,000	Right	9,000
Right	9,000	Left	8,000
		Far left	2,000

If a party of the centre intervenes, the effect may be equally perverse. If the centre candidate leans more to the right than the left, as in Example 2, Table 2.2, by a ratio of 2:1, then it may help the left.

TABLE 2.2 **EXAMPLE 2**

Election 1		*Election 2*	
Right	10,000	Left	8,500
Left	9,500	Right	8,000
		Centre	3,000

There is also the "third-party squeeze". Voters on the left, finding themselves in third place and believing their candidate will never win, may decide to cut their losses and switch to the centre to beat the right.

TABLE 2.3   **EXAMPLE 3**

Election 1		*Election 2*	
Right	9,000	Centre	10,000
Centre	6,000	Right	9,000
Left	5,000	Left	1,000

The most obvious failing in FPTP is where the result can depend on which parties put up candidates. This can be seen very clearly in Northern Ireland seats. There is little change in the overall Unionist or nationalist vote from one election to the next and both sides' chances depend on being able to field a single candidate. A good example is the old Mid Ulster constituency which had a small nationalist majority and was held by Bernadette Devlin from 1969 to 1974 but since then has had a Unionist MP. The seat was considerably redrawn at the last election to give it a much larger nationalist majority and it was won by Martin McGuinness for Sinn Fein. But in the previous six elections a split in the nationalist vote between the Social Democratic & Labour Party and republican candidates handed the seat to the Unionists, although a split in the Unionist vote nearly handed it back to the nationalists in 1983.

This splitting the vote problem has led to cases where candidates have been physically threatened on the way to hand in nomination papers. There have been secret deals between parties to share out seats over the heads of the voters and there have been tacit electoral pacts – most controversially in Berkshire in the county council elections of 1993 – where one local party decided off its own bat not to put up candidates in certain seats. All of this derives from the incapacity of the system to deal with a situation that was rare in the 19th century but is universal now where more than two candidates are nominated for the same seat.

TABLE 2.4   MID ULSTER: PERCENTAGE VOTE

	1992	1987	1983	1979	1974
Unionist	42	44	30	45	47
Other Unionist	–	–	13	–	–
SDLP	31	26	22	29	40
Republican	19	24	29.9	18	13
Other Republican	–	2	1	2	–
Other	7	4	3	5	–
All Unionist	**42**	**44**	**43**	**45**	**47**
All Nationalist	**50**	**52**	**52**	**49**	**53**

The perverse feature of the split vote is that there are people who say after the election that they would have voted differently if they had known what the result was going to be. In Table 2.1, there are bound to be 1,001 of the far left voters who would have voted left if they had known they were letting the right in. In Example 2 there will probably be at least 501 centre party voters who regret having 'let the left in'. The system means that some voters need to know the result before they know how to vote. That also means that they can be influenced by opinion polls or indeed by any figures purporting to be opinion polls put out by the political parties. It has been a common by-election tactic for parties to put out opinion poll figures showing their candidate in second place in order to encourage tactical voters to switch to them.

This is a technique which works only because of the inability of FPTP to cope with more than two candidates and the way it creates a need for some voters to second-guess the result. The third-party squeeze is what happens when people do vote differently because they thought they knew what the result was going to be. Sometimes their vote makes no difference and they wish they had not switched, but on other occasions they are glad they did, because their tactical vote defeated the candidates they wanted to stop.

A classic case of third-party squeeze occurred when the 1997 Winchester election was re-run after a Liberal Democrat victory over the

Conservative by two votes was declared void. In the re-run, Labour voters flocked to the Liberal Democrat candidate in order to beat the Conservatives even though it resulted in the Labour candidate losing his deposit.

What is clear, however, is that the more candidates stand in a constituency the more the distortions inherent in the system are encouraging voters to engage in tactics and in guesswork rather than voting positively for the party they support.

But there is an even more fundamental drawback in FPTP or indeed any majoritarian voting system. It represents territories, not voters. Voters are represented only if they happen to form the majority in a territory. Voters who are in a minority are represented only in the formal sense that they have an MP, but their opinions are not represented. It must seem perverse to a mathematician to use territorial representation to measure opinions that do not follow territorial lines. The result will be determined not only by the strength of different opinions but also by their geographical distribution. This is why a party that wins the most votes can still be defeated by another party that wins fewer votes but more seats. Indeed, this happened to the Labour Party in 1951 and to the Conservative Party in February 1974. In theory a party can win 51 per cent of the votes in 51 per cent of the constituencies and win a majority in parliament, even though it has only just over a quarter of the votes. Indeed under the FPTP system there can be even stranger results. If there are three candidates in every constituency, a party could win with just 34 per cent of the vote in half the constituencies, ie 17 per cent. This would be a freak result, but this distortion caused by the distribution of votes is bound to exist to some degree in any territorial election.

It is this distortion, this disproportionality, that provides the primary theoretical objection to FPTP. But a more serious flaw in the system may be the lack of any clear causative link between voting and representation. In other voting systems almost every vote helps to elect an MP, so every voter is represented in parliament. In FPTP only the votes cast for successful candidates count and even then many of them are superfluous if the MP has a large majority. Most voters do not have an MP whom they have helped to elect and who represents their views.

Following the 1997 election the biases of FPTP have been examined again. One startling fact this has revealed is that Labour would have an 82-seat majority in the House of Commons if it and the Conservatives had got the same number of votes. If 6.5 per cent of the vote was taken from Labour and given to the Conservatives, both parties would have the same share of the vote, 37 per cent. Labour would win extra seats by distributing its 37 per cent across seats that mattered, the marginal constituencies. Ron Johnston, Professor of Geography at the University of Bristol, speaking of his findings at a conference in January 1998, gave the credit to Peter Mandelson for targeting key smaller seats and gaining an advantage out of proportion to Labour's votes.

During the election, the *Independent* headline, "Just 70,000 targeted: what about the election's neglected millions", made people think – many for the first time – how with modern technology and targeting, elections can be won without the majority of us being involved. Not only do party campaigners work hardest in their target seats but also policy can be drafted to win the voters who need to switch to give the party the majority they require. One leadership visit to South Dorset might have given Labour the seat but when the election was called the Labour leader went straight to Worcester which was the target seat which would give Labour its majority.

The voting system distorts the way parties behave and manifestos and policies are decided, and the outcome of an election is determined by the geographical spread of parties rather than their actual support. Distortions can reinforce each other in the same direction as they mainly did in 1997 but they are still there inherent in the voting system. Sometimes the biases cancel each other out. But the best way to create a better politics is to ensure that the system contains as few biases as possible. This is very difficult to do in a purely constituency-based system.

3 DISILLUSION

The sense that your vote is wasted may exist even when there are only two parties, if one of them seems certain to win. Walter Bagehot, the first and still in many ways the most effective defender of the current voting system, conceded that this was one of its failings when he wrote in *The English Constitution* in 1873: "I have myself had a vote for an agricultural county for 20 years and I am a Liberal; but two Tories have always been returned and all my life will be returned."

He treated it as no more than a minor blemish on the system that many voters would be condemned to a lifetime of futility and frustration by the accident of being Liberals living in Tory areas or Tories living in Liberal areas. The point for Bagehot was not whether his individual vote counted, but whether the collective will of the voters was translated into effective government.

It is this fault, however, that has done more than anything else to unravel support for the system. The system works for Tories who live in Tory areas, for Liberal Democrats who live in Liberal Democrat areas and for Labour voters who live in Labour areas. Even if they do not vote for the party in government, they can be confident that their votes count towards the result of the election and help to elect someone who will represent them in parliament. But an increasing proportion of the electorate feel that their votes do not count and that their MPs, although able to help on personal matters, do not represent them politically.

There are 130,916 Labour voters in Surrey but they have no Labour MPs and they never have had. Considering that they failed to win a single seat in 1997, they would need to be inveterate optimists to convince themselves that they ever will. In fact the majority of Labour candidates in Surrey failed even to lift themselves into second place in Labour's best election since 1945. There are 141,120 Conservative voters in Merseyside and they do not have a single Conservative MP. Indeed in Liverpool no Conservative candidate even made second place in 1997. So the Surrey Socialist and the Scouse Tory are in rather similar positions. If they had stayed at home on polling day, it would not have made any possible difference to the result nationally or locally. They would be unlikely even to have had the satisfaction of reducing the other party's majority by one. It is a feeling of complete impotence to be a Labour voter in Surrey Heath and to know that your Conservative MP has a majority of 16,287 over the Liberal Democrat in second place, or to be a Tory voter in Liverpool Walton and to know that your Labour MP has a majority of 27,038 over the Liberal Democrat, with your candidate in third place. It is astonishing in the circumstances that people vote at all.

TABLE 3.1 **WASTED AND SUPERFLUOUS VOTES, 1992 AND 1997**

	1992			1997		
	Wasted votes	Super-fluous votes	Total %	Wasted votes	Super-fluous votes	Total %
Con	369,735	3,938,198	30.6	430,611	1,087,670	15.8
Lab	1,417,813	2,811,067	36.6	1,126,862	5,549,621	49.3
Lib Dem	2,910,169	80,543	49.9	2,791,217	240,225	57.8

The definition of a wasted vote varies. Votes for candidates who come third or lower are obviously wasted. In a logical sense votes for the second candidate are not wasted, because they are the post that the winning candidate has to get past. If a candidate wins by 20,000 votes to 19,999, then every voter can feel that their vote counted. Any one of those voters can feel that if they had not voted the way they did, or if they had changed their mind, the result would have been different.

But the problem of wasted votes is much wider than that. In an article entitled "Votes that Count and Votes that Don't", Ron Johnston, Charles Pattie and David Rossiter distinguish between wasted votes, surplus votes and effective votes. Wasted votes are considered to be all the votes cast for defeated candidates. Surplus votes are those cast for winning candidates over and above what they need in order to win. Effective votes are those cast for winning candidates that they actually need to be elected, that is, as many as the second placed candidate plus one.

TABLE 3.2   **WASTED, SURPLUS AND EFFECTIVE VOTES, 1997**

	Wasted votes[a]	%	Surplus votes[a]	%	Effective votes[a]	%	Votes in GB
Con	5,741,000	60	1,088,000	11	2,763,000	29	9,591,082
Lab	2,809,000	21	5,550,000	41	5,159,000	38	13,517,911
Lib Dem	4,231,000	81	240,000	5	773,000	15	5,243,440
Others	1,914,000	89	92,000	4	139,000	6	2,144,491
Total	**14,694,000**	**48**	**6,969,000**	**22**	**8,834,000**	**29**	**30,496,924**

a   Rounded to the nearest '000.

Table 3.2 shows just how far the UK's electoral system has to go before it achieves the modest aim that is the title of this book, *Making Votes Count*. Nearly 15 million votes were wasted and the voters that cast them are therefore not represented by an MP of the party they voted for. Nearly 7 million votes were just piled up in surplus majorities, or vote mountains, for winning candidates. Only just over a quarter of the votes were necessary to elect the candidates who were elected.

The number of wasted votes was highest among voters for other parties, 89 per cent, and Liberal Democrats, 81 per cent, and perversely they are the votes which have increased most rapidly over the last few decades. Between 1951 and 1983, third and minor-party support increased ninefold from 3.3 per cent to 30 per cent , and it has remained high since, with 26 per cent of the vote in 1997. To put it the other way round, the percentage voting for the two main parties has fallen from very nearly everyone, 96.7 per cent, to less than three in four, 74 per cent. Why do people vote for parties which cannot form governments? Only a small part of this can be accounted for by protest votes or votes by committed supporters of parties which stand no chance of success, such as the Referendum and UK Independence parties or the parties of extreme right or left, or votes for joke parties like the Monster Raving Loony Party. The great majority comes from the rise in support for the very parties that have a very high percentage of wasted votes, the Liberal Democrats and the nationalist parties.

One might have expected that a voting system that works best when there are only two candidates in each constituency and only two parties in parliament would tend to encourage people to vote for one of the main parties and squeeze out third parties. But the opposite has happened. As Table 3.3 shows, the proportion voting for the two main parties has fallen, while the proportion voting for smaller parties has grown correspondingly.

TABLE 3.3   **% VOTES CAST FOR THE TWO MAIN PARTIES, 1951–97**

1951	1964	1983	1992	1997
96.7	87.5	70.0	76.3	73.9

Another example of this perversity has been in the reduction in the number of majority mandates. As Table 3.4 shows, 94 percent of MPs elected in 1951 could claim that more than half of their constituents who voted had voted for them. They knew, of course, that first-past-the-post (FPTP) was not a genuine majoritarian system that required MPs to win a majority of votes but simply a plurality system that required them only to win more votes than their rivals. But it might have made little difference if that election had been fought on a preferential voting system, like the alternative vote (AV), as only a handful of seats would have needed to go to a second round. Since 1951 the proportion of MPs with majority mandates has fallen steadily to 51 per cent in 1997.

TABLE 3.4   MPS ELECTED ON MAJORITY MANDATES, 1951–97

	1951	1964	1983	1992	1997
No.	586	398	314	392	339
%	94	63	60	60	51

This undermines the standing of MPs. Just as governments have less legitimacy when they have been elected with a low share of the popular vote, so MPs speak with less authority both in their constituency and in parliament if they are elected, as sometimes happens, with the support of only around one-third of their constituents. As Table 3.5 shows, the trend towards lower turnouts in general elections means that even fewer MPs can claim nowadays to have the support of a majority of their constituents (including those who did not vote). In 1992 only 34 MPs could claim that a majority of their electorate voted for them and in 1997 it was only 14. This is bizarre in a country where so much importance is attached to the MP's role as a representative. Writing to and going to see one's MP are seen almost as a constitutional right.

TABLE 3.5   MPS SUPPORTED BY MAJORITY OF ELECTORS, 1951–97

	1951	1964	1983	1992	1997
No.	214	54	1	34	14
%	34	9	0.2	5	2

It is one of the advantages of the second ballot used in France that the winner of the election must, by definition, have the support of the majority of voters, and that confers much greater legitimacy than a FPTP election. François Mitterrand, for instance, was elected by 51 per cent of the French voters whereas Margaret Thatcher never received more than 43 per cent of the vote. That does not necessarily mean that President Mitterrand was more popular than Prime Minister Thatcher. The difference is inherent in the voting systems. But it does point to the way that the FPTP system, combined with a falling turnout in elections which has itself been partly caused by FPTP, has undermined the legitimacy of MPs. Although some MPs enjoy very high support, the average vote for an MP as a percentage of the electorate in their constituency is usually less than two-fifths.

TABLE 3.6 **% ELECTORS WHO VOTED FOR THEIR LOCAL MP, 1979–97**

1979	1983	1987	1992	1997
39	36	39	41	37

In 1992 a Scottish Liberal Democrat, Sir Russell Johnston, was elected by just 26 per cent of the voters. Thus 74 per cent of the voters in his seat, Inverness, Nairn & Lochaber, did not vote Liberal Democrat, yet had a Liberal Democrat MP. As a percentage of the electorate the Liberal Democrat vote was only 19 per cent and, allowing for the normal turnover of electors, it was probably little over 14 per cent by the end of that parliament.

TABLE 3.7 **INVERNESS, NAIRN & LOCHABER, 1992**

	Lib Dem	Lab	SNP	Con
% voters	26.0	25.1	24.7	22.6
% electors	19.1	18.4	18.1	16.6

This may help to explain how the Labour candidate David Stewart, a Labour Campaign for Electoral Reform sponsor, came from notional fourth place in 1992 to win the slightly redrawn seat of Inverness East,

Nairn & Lochaber in 1997, and the Liberal Democrat candidate Stephen Gallagher went from first to third, only just avoiding fourth place. It was one of the few four-way marginals in 1997. The lowest winning share in the 1997 election was for Michael Moore who won Tweeddale, Ettrick & Lauderdale with less than a third of the vote and less than a quarter of the electorate.

TABLE 3.8   **TWEEDDALE, ETTRICK & LAUDERDALE, 1997**

	Lib Dem	*Lab*	*SNP*	*Con*
% voters	31.2	27.4	17.1	22.1
% electors	23.9	21.0	13.1	16.9

One of the problems of the FPTP system is that it is theoretically possible to win a seat on any share of the vote, no matter how low. If there are three candidates, one could win on 34 per cent. If there are four, one could win on 26 per cent. If five, 21 per cent. If there were 21 candidates who all won 4.6–4.9 per cent of the vote, it would be possible for a candidate to be declared elected and at the same time lose the deposit which is automatically forfeited by any candidate who wins less than 5 per cent of the vote. This seems inconceivable, but in the 1950s no one would have believed that an MP would be elected on 26 per cent of the vote.

What applies to the election of candidates under FPTP must also apply to the election of governments. No post-war government has been able to claim the support of two-fifths of the electorate, though ironically Labour had the support of over two-fifths of the electorate in 1951 – and lost. In the last seven elections the government has had the support of less than a third of the electorate, although Margaret Thatcher came very close in 1979.

TABLE 3.9 % ELECTORS WHO VOTED FOR THE
          GOVERNMENT, 1951–97

	1951	1966	1974 Oct	1979	1983	1987	1992	1997
%	39.6	36.4	28.6	33.3	30.8	31.9	32.6	30.9

The proportion of electors who exercise their vote in general elections has decreased since the immediate post-war years, even though
the choice of candidates is much wider. It is not right to describe all
those who do not vote as abstainers. Some have moved since the register was compiled (although they are entitled to a postal vote), some
are registered in two places (and can vote in only one), some are put on
or left off the voting register by mistake and some have died since the
electoral register came into force. Richard Rose compiled adjusted figures for non-voters in his book *Electoral Behaviour*, taking account of
those who had died or moved since the electoral register was compiled,
but even on this basis Britain has one of the highest levels of non-
voting in Europe and the trend is upwards. And this is despite the fact
that the rules have been relaxed to make it easier to qualify for a postal
vote and to allow people to put their names on the electoral register at
any time of year (instead of just in October).

TABLE 3.10   NON-VOTERS, 1950–97

	No.	%	Adjusted %[a]
1950	5,540373	16.1	13.1
1951	6,075,963	17.4	8.3
1964	8,219,739	22.9	14.3
1970	11,015,763	28.0	23.0
1983	11,518,688	27.3	22.2
1992	9,642,281	22.3	18.0
1997	12,496,857	28.5	24.6

a Figures from *Britain Votes 1997*.

The turnout was lower in 1997 than at any general election since 1935. Some of this may have been because of what seemed from the polls to be the inevitability of the result. Some of it may have been because the election was so focused on marginal seats. What many people thought might have led to disillusion and low turnout was summed up by the introduction to *The Vacher Dod Guide to the New House of Commons*, which said that the campaign was "aimed at identified groups of voters in marginal seats, a mere 0.25 per cent of the entire electorate. It was certainly very difficult to see this so-called 'professionalisation' of politics as an enhancement of democracy, and much easier to see it as a way of draining genuine debate from the campaign."

But what may be as important as the number of electors who fail to vote is the number of people who are not registered at all. The poll tax undoubtedly affected the efficiency of electoral registers for the 1992 general election. This can be seen by comparing the number on electoral registers and the Registrar-General's census estimate of the number of people aged over 18. Although the figures should not be identical because some people do not qualify for the electoral register, the shortfall should not be very great and should not vary much over time. It was 1 million in 1987 and went up to 1.8 million in 1992. The Office of Population, Census and Surveys (OPCS) estimated that 2.2 million (4.8 per cent) of the people documented in the 1991 census were not on the electoral roll. These were not evenly distributed across the population or the country: people under 24 were twice as likely to be unregistered as those over 50; inner London residents three times as likely as those in non-metropolitan areas; people who had moved in the last year five times as likely as those who had not; New Commonwealth citizens six times as likely as the rest and those living in private, furnished accommodation 15 times as likely as owner-occupiers.

Professor Iain McLean of Oxford University has estimated that this deregistration handed an extra nine seats to the Conservatives in 1992. Although the poll tax has been replaced by the council tax, there may have been continuing under-registration by those who believed that identifying themselves and their addresses in a public document might make them liable for council tax or who had just got into the habit of not registering during the time of the poll tax. This also has another effect. The job of the boundary commissions is to equalise the number of people living in each constituency on the basis of current electorates every 8–12 years. That means that any deregistration will be embedded in the system as under-representation for the next decade. It is unfortunate that the last boundary review began in 1991 and used the electoral registers of 1991, the year when the register was most out of kilter with the census estimate because of the poll tax.

Another result of FPTP, or indeed any majoritarian system is that the likely result in a particular constituency is often predetermined by the boundary review which decides where the boundaries are drawn long before candidates are chosen or votes cast. Nothing can be more disillusioning about elections than attending an inquiry of the boundary commission and witnessing the earnestness with which local clergymen and others put up by the political parties put their arguments about school catchment areas, natural communities and bus routes. In the former county of Avon, deregistration was a factor which led the Boundary Inquiry to support the Conservative and Labour proposal to keep 10 constituencies rather than the Liberal Democrat proposal to create 11. Although the results in 1997 serve to reinforce the idea that when the Conservatives drop below one-third of the vote, their representation collapses, the decisions taken at the Boundary Inquiry would have helped to determine the result in a closer run election. Table 3.11 shows the votes and the seats won by the three main parties in the last two elections.

TABLE 3.11 **VOTES AND SEATS IN AVON, 1992 & 1997**

	1992			1997		
	Votes	*%*	*Seats*	*Votes*	*%*	*Seats*
Con	261,772	44.5	6	181,606	32.7	1
Lab	161,952	27.5	3	202,778	36.5	6
Lib Dem	155,663	26.5	1	146,270	26.3	3

As can be seen from the above correlation between votes and seats, FPTP has never made much sense as a theory of representation. It has the effect that most people are represented in parliament by MPs they did not vote for and MPs represent electors who largely did not vote for them. Three-quarters of the voters of Tweeddale, Ettrick & Lauderdale did not vote for the Liberal Democrats, yet they have a Liberal Democrat MP. But four-fifths of the people who did vote Liberal Democrat in the rest of the country in 1997 did not get a Liberal Democrat MP. There is a mismatch between people who vote Liberal Democrat and people who have Liberal Democrat MPs. Scotland and the South-west accounted for more than 50 per cent of their MPs but less than 25 per cent of their votes. The rest of the country provided three-quarters of their vote but won less than half their seats. Why deny Liberal Democrat MPs to so many people who do vote for them and why impose Liberal Democrat MPs on so many people who do not?

The link between MPs and constituents is not nearly as strong as MPs would like to think. MPs are fond of saying that they represent not only the people who voted for them but all of their constituents. That is a fine sentiment. If it means that they will help any constituent with a personal problem, regardless of how they vote, then it is a good principle. If it means that they will speak for all their constituents on matters of local or regional interest, defending the interests of a local industry, expressing the grief of a community after a tragedy, then it is a necessary role. But in so far as MPs are elected to represent views on national issues, and that is their main function, they cannot represent the view of all their constituents. There is no typically Hartlepool view on events in the Middle East. There is no typically Cornish view on the single currency. MPs represent people who hold contradictory views. They can say different things to different people to keep them happy, but they cannot vote in different ways on the same bill or the same vote of confidence.

Nor do voters see their votes translated into representation. It has long been the case that a vote for the Liberals is likely to be wasted in most constituencies, but the disease also affects Labour and Conservative voters. As Table 3.12 shows, more than 6 million voters live in constituencies where Labour candidates came not only third but a poor third (at least 20 per cent behind the leading party) thus having little immediate prospect of winning the seat. Even in the 1997 landslide, there were 221 Labour candidates who failed to be elected. Another 5 million voters live in seats where Conservative candidates came a poor third (see Table 3.13 on the following page). The position has improved for Labour since a low point in 1983, but in 1997 Conservative and Labour voters were effectively "disenfranchised" in 13–14 per cent of seats.

TABLE 3.12   **DISENFRANCHISEMENT OF POTENTIAL LABOUR VOTERS: CONSTITUENCIES WHERE LABOUR IS IN 3RD PLACE OR LOWER**

	3rd place	Poor 3rd[a]	% seats where Lab poor 3rd	Total voters where Lab poor 3rd
1955	12	11	2	500,000
1959	27	26	4	1,200,000
1964	52	46	7	2,200,000
1966	31	24	4	1,100,000
1970	34	30	5	1,600,000
1974 Feb	149	123	19	6,500,000
1974 Oct	115	95	15	5,000,000
1979	99	95	15	5,200,000
1983	292	274	42	17,800,000
1987	255	242	37	16,100,000
1992	171	161	25	10,800,000
1997	120	95	14	6,300,000

a At least 20 per cent behind winning candidate.

TABLE 3.13   DISENFRANCHISEMENT OF POTENTIAL
              CONSERVATIVE VOTERS: CONSTITUENCIES
              WHERE CONSERVATIVES ARE IN 3RD
              PLACE OR LOWER

	3rd place	Poor 3rd[a]	% seats where Con poor 3rd	Total voters where Con poor 3rd
1955	11	11	2	500,000
1959	10	9	1	400,000
1964	14	11	2	500,000
1966	15	12	2	600,000
1970	20	16	3	800,000
1974 Feb	45	37	6	2,000,000
1974 Oct	65	58	9	3,100,000
1979	15	11	2	600,000
1983	55	45	7	2,900,000
1987	48	42	6	2,800,000
1992	52	47	7	3,100,000
1997	90	83	13	5,500,000

a At least 20 per cent behind winning candidate.

In brief, people are now less likely to have voted for their local MP,
less likely to have voted for the governing party, less likely to have
voted for one of the two main parties, less likely to have voted at all,
less likely to be registered to vote, and MPs are less likely to have the
support of a majority of their voters or their constituents. More and
more people feel they have no part to play in elections. They have less
sense of ownership of the political process. It is no exaggeration to describe this as a sense of disenfranchisement.

4 TACTICALISATION

In order to understand what is happening in our FPTP elections it is perhaps useful to distinguish between two models of voting behaviour. Under the old model people vote for the party that expresses their view, regardless of whether the candidate has any chance of winning in their constituency or not. If they are Tory, they vote Tory, if they are Labour, they vote Labour, and that's that. This expressive model is taught in the textbooks and is assumed to exist in the mind of the voter when academics, commentators and pollsters apply a universal swing to all seats in an election. It is also the model that supporters of a party follow if they have the good fortune to live in seats which are held by or are winnable for that party.

But there is now a new model of voting. Whom you vote for depends on who is likely to win in your seat. You vote in a way that will be effective and if you are unable to do that, you may not vote at all. The expressive model appeals to traditional virtues such as loyalty and fidelity. Voting is like going to church: it is an expression of faith. Even if your local candidate has no chance of winning, you can console yourself with the thought that there will be an equal number of wasted votes on the other side and the result will probably reflect the overall balance of opinion in the country.

The new rational model, on the other hand, is streetwise, proactive, individualised. Voting is more like going to a shop, a contract between a buyer and a seller. You do not accept a wasted vote any more than you accept shoddy goods. You expect your vote to give you some purchase on the choice of government. If a vote for your first-choice party does not achieve this, you cast your vote in a tactical way to defeat the party you do not want and thus help your own party into power.

In the 1950s almost everyone voted on the expressive model. They voted for what they believed in if they could. There were many seats where the Liberals did not stand and the voters were forced to choose between Conservative and Labour. There were just a smattering of seats where Labour came a poor third and the real choice was between Conservative and Liberal: these were Dorset North, the seat of the Liberal Whip Frank Byers, Eye in rural Suffolk, Honiton in Devon, Westmorland, Bodmin and Cornwall North. At the time this was attributed to a Liberal tradition in those areas, but with hindsight it is clear that Labour voters in these seats were making a tactical decision to vote Liberal.

Although we still have the same voting system as in the 1950s, we do not vote in the same way. We have shifted gradually, almost imperceptibly, from the old model to the new. The new model made its first appearance in parliamentary by-elections. We will see in Chapter 10, the history of the 'golden era', how the Liberals came from nowhere to win second place in the 1954 Inverness by-election and then won the Torrington by-election in Devon in 1958 and the Orpington by-election in Kent in 1962, demonstrating their ability to squeeze the vote of other parties.

The next elections to witness the effect of third-party squeeze were local elections, where the Liberals took Conservative seats with the help of Labour voters and Labour seats with the help of Conservative voters. General elections were the last to feel the impact of new model voting, but the effect has nevertheless been profound. Millions of voters have suspended normal allegiances in order to make their votes count. They have started voting with their heads instead of their hearts.

There is, however, an imbalance between the parties. Labour voters have moved over much more quickly and more completely to the new model. For some reason Labour supporters gang up with the Liberals to get the Tory out more often than the Tories gang up with the Liberals to get Labour out. There are exceptions, of course, such as the Bermondsey by-election of 1983, when Tory voters switched to Liberal to help win Labour's then third safest London seat. There is also the unusual history of Colne Valley where Tory supporters used to vote Liberal to keep Labour out. But while Conservatives have been just as keen to use protest voting in by-elections and European elections, they have been far less likely than Labour supporters to engage in tactical voting in parliamentary elections. This is why the Conservatives have lost far more seats to the Liberals than the Labour Party has. Of the 46 seats currently held by the Liberal Democrats, only two were originally won from Labour (Bermondsey, Caithness & Sutherland), two can be described as traditional Liberal seats, Montgomeryshire and Orkney & Shetland, and the remaining 42 were all won at some point from the Conservatives.

But, almost unnoticed in the 1997 election, the Liberal Democrats have started moving into second place behind Labour in some northern cities. In the past they have usually had one isolated outpost in each city: Edgehill (Mossley Hill) in Liverpool, Yardley in Birmingham, Hillsborough/Hallam in Sheffield and Leeds West, which they had been able to build up by concentrating their resources. But in 1997 they began to emerge as the major opposition to Labour in the big cities, beating the Conservatives into third or fourth place in every Labour-held seat in Liverpool and in most seats in Sheffield and Manchester. This may have been caused by the weakening of the Conservative vote rather than by any conscious tactical voting by Conservatives but it nevertheless leaves a very different tactical situation facing voters at the next election. They may judge that the best way to vote against Labour in the inner cities at the next election may be to vote Liberal Democrat. That will leave the Conservatives trapped in third place with their vote just as vulnerable to third-party squeeze as the Labour vote has been in strongly agricultural seats.

Not only did the Conservatives fall from first place to second place in all the seats they lost in 1997, they fell from second to third place in a lot more. In fact they nearly doubled the number of seats in Britain where they are in third place or lower. If they cannot get back into contention in the next election, they may find their vote held down by a ratchet in the same way that Labour was in the 1980s. That in turn will reduce the overall share of vote that they win for any given number of seats and that can have damaging effects on the self-confidence of the party.

But it may do even more to undermine Conservative confidence in the voting system. The reason why they have had such faith in the system up to now is not just because they have won the majority of elections but because the Conservative candidate has come first or second in nearly every seat (92 per cent in 1992). That makes it reasonable to think of the battle between two candidates for a seat as a proxy for the battle between two parties for power. It gives credibility to the idea that voters are exercising not just a choice of an MP for their constituency but a choice of government for their country. But the proportion of voters who will have a Conservative in first or second place in their constituencies in the next election will be only 86 per cent and the proportion who will have Labour in first or second place will be 81 per cent. The proportion who will actually have a straight Conservative-Labour fight in their constituencies will be only two thirds. So assuming that the effective choice of government is still between Conservative and Labour, one voter in three in Britain (and all the voters in Northern Ireland) will face a choice of effective contenders in their constituency which is different from the choice of government and therefore gives them no direct purchase on the choice of government.

TABLE 4.1   **NON CONSERVATIVE–LABOUR SEATS, 1992 AND 1997**

Lab 3rd/4th behind	1992	1997	Con 3rd/4th behind	1992	1997
Con & Lib Dem	148	73	Lab & Lib Dem	8	30
Lib Dem & Con	16	39	Lib Dem & Lab	4	6
Con & SNP	3	–	Lab & SNP	32	43
Con & PC	3	–	Lab & PC	2	4
SNP & Con	3	6	SNP & Lab	–	–
PC & Con	3	–	Lab & Other	3	1
			PC & Lab	–	4
Total	**176**	**118**	**Total**	**49**	**88**

There was one seat where Labour and Conservative were in third and fourth place in 1992, behind Plaid Cymru and the Liberal Democrats. After the 1992 election, Labour was in third place or lower in more than three times as many seats as the Conservatives. Labour was in third place or lower in 176 seats, the Conservatives only in 49. Thus there were far more opportunities for Liberal Democrats to squeeze Labour votes than to squeeze Conservative votes. After 1997 Labour was in third place or lower in 119 seats, Conservative in 89. In Argyll & Bute, both came behind the Liberal Democrat and the SNP. Considering the Labour Party had just had its best election vote ever, the only surprise was that it was still in third place in any seat. That can only be explained if many of the people who would have voted Labour decided, for tactical reasons, to vote for another party that stood a better chance of beating the Tories.

To find out why Labour voters should still be more willing than their Conservative counterparts to engage in tactical voting would require a long-term study of voter psychology. Is it because Labour supporters are more fickle than Tory? Or because they are more ruthless? Because they were less firmly attached to Labour in the first place? Or because they are more subtle in their manipulation of the voting system? Or because Labour heartlands are stronger than Conservative heartlands? Or after 18 years of opposition to Conservative governments, Labour and Liberal Democrat policy was perceived to be sufficiently similar to allow votes to be exchanged? All that is clear is that over the last 40 years the behaviour of Labour supporters in Tory strongholds has differed from that of Tory supporters in Labour strongholds.

That may be changing. But the results in May 1997 still show the two-party battlefield. The different behaviour of Labour and Conservative supporters can be seen in the two examples in Table 4.2 on the following page. Labour never had any realistic chance of winning the Isle of Wight. The closest they came was in 1945 when they took 41 per cent of the vote, but after that the Labour vote went down, helped by the closure of factories on the island. The Liberals did not put up candidates in 1951, 1955 and 1959, but in the 1960s they reappeared

TABLE 4.2   **ISLE OF WIGHT AND
                   HEMSWORTH VOTERS, 1950–1997**

	Isle of Wight		Hemsworth	
	Lab	%	Con	%
1950	21,496	40	10,254	18
1951	20,712	38	9,911	17
1955	18,698	37	8,561	17
1959	18,396	37	9,788	18
1964	16,244	32	8,668	17
1966	15,411	29	7,165	15
1970	13,111	23	9,534	19
1974 Feb	7,495	11	9,152	17
1974 Oct	8,562	13	5,895	12
1979	3,014	4	10,466	20
1983	1,828	2	7,891	21
1987	4,626	6	7,159	17
1992	4,784	6	7,867	19
1997	9,646	13	8,096	18

and gradually replaced Labour as the opposition to the Tories. In 1974 the Liberals leapfrogged from third place to win the seat by pushing the Labour vote down sharply from 13,111 to 7,495. In ensuing elections they squeezed Labour's vote down to 1,828 in 1983, the lowest vote Labour recorded in a post-war parliamentary election until the Newbury by-election in 1993. It was widely assumed that the fall in Labour's vote in seats like the Isle of Wight was a result of demographic changes, but demographic change, while it has undoubtedly been significant, cannot explain more than a fraction of the fall in Labour's vote from 40 to 2 per cent. The truth is that former Labour voters in the Isle of Wight switched to the Liberals as an alternative opposition party that was more likely to win the seat from the Tories, and they were right.

Tory supporters were even more of a lost cause in the Labour mining stronghold of Hemsworth in Yorkshire, but unlike Labour supporters on the Isle of Wight they stuck to their party. The Tories won
a remarkably consistent 17–19 per cent of the vote, which is where
they remain today. Which group of supporters was right? One could
argue that the Hemsworth Tories were more realistic. They were never
going to beat Labour, which sometimes had over 80 per cent of the
vote. So their only strategy was to keep voting Tory and to ignore all
distractions. In the by-election in 1991, the Liberal Democrats tried
hard and managed to get into second place, but they were still so far
behind Labour that they were clearly not going to win the seat. At the
1992 election the Tories were back in second place with their traditional share of the vote, where they remained in 1997.

Isle of Wight Labour supporters could have taken the same attitude.
Labour was never going to win and it did not look as though the Tories
could ever lose. They had more than 60 per cent of the vote throughout the 1950s. Nevertheless, the Liberals came from nowhere to first
place in ten years, which they could not have done without the defec-
tion of seven out of ten and eventually 19 out of 20 Labour voters.
That resulted in the first defeat the Tories had sustained on the island
since 1923. The psephologist Michael Steed has estimated that the Tories lost three safe seats to the Liberals as a result of tactical voting in
February 1974. In most elections this would be unimportant, but the
February 1974 election was so close that it may have played a role in
the post-election arithmetic. The Conservatives ended up as the second
largest party with 297 seats. The prime minister, Edward Heath, stayed
in Downing Street after the election trying to win enough support
from smaller parties to take him past the magic number of 318 which
would have given him a majority. If he had won the support of the Ulster Unionists, the SNP and Plaid Cymru, that would have left him with
only 317, one short of a majority. He was thus forced to turn to the
Liberals who held the balance of power. They, after some prevarication,
turned him down. As a result Labour's Harold Wilson was asked to
form a government. The former Labour voters of the Isle of Wight

played their part in this. If they had not switched to the Liberals in such numbers, the Conservatives would have held the Isle of Wight and then they could have formed a majority with the Unionists and nationalists. So, although the Liberals won the seat, the effect was to put Labour back in power. The action of Labour supporters in deserting the Labour Party in the Isle of Wight helped to ensure, paradoxically, that Labour formed the 1974–79 Government.

The Isle of Wight is taken as an example because it is the only seat in England whose boundaries have not been changed by the boundary commission. In every other seat changes in the vote may be explained to some extent by boundary changes or demographic changes. But one only needs to compare election results from the 1950s and the 1980s or 1990s to see that what has happened on the Isle of Wight has happened to some degree in the whole of rural England and across the South, excluding only the larger cities. The three seats in Table 4.3 opposite, Wilts North, Cheltenham and Newbury, have behaved in the same way: once the Labour vote has fallen below the Liberal vote, it drops sharply as the Liberals apply a third-party squeeze on Labour, but if the Liberals fail to take the seat when Labour has been squeezed down to its core vote, then the Labour vote starts to revive.

It is striking how much more sharply the Labour vote fell in these seats than in the country as a whole in the 1970s and 1980s. The Labour votes were 4, 5 and 6 percentage points behind Labour's national vote in 1951, but were 20–30 percentage points behind in the last three elections. The Labour vote reached its low point in Chippenham in 1983, the year when the Liberals were confident of taking the seat, but since they failed, some of the tactical voters have started drifting back to Labour over the last three elections.

In Cheltenham and Newbury the Liberal Democrats succeeded in squeezing the Labour vote a little further to win both seats, Cheltenham in the 1992 election and Newbury in a by-election the following year. As a result there are very few Labour voters left. For every ten people who voted Labour in 1951, seven have now switched to another party in Chippenham and nine have switched in Newbury.

TABLE 4.3   DECLINE OF LABOUR VOTE IN
             UNWINNABLE SEATS

	Wilts North[a]		Cheltenham		Newbury		UK
	Lab	%	Lab	%	Lab	%	%
1951	17,723	44	17,777	43	13,507	40	49
1955	14,152	35	16,638	41	18,843	42	46
1959	12,911	31	12,725	30	19,787	40	44
1964	10,086	23[b]	14,557	35	18,943	34	44
1966	10,257	22[b]	19,768	47	21,762	38	48
1970	10,807	22[b]	14,213	31	18,647	30	43
1974 Feb	9,395	17[b]	12,971	26[b]	10,035	17[b]	37
1974 Oct	9,396	18[b]	12,134	26[b]	9,390	17[b]	39
1979	5,146	9[b]	9,185	18[b]	6,676	11[b]	37
1983	2,888	5[b]	4,390	8[b]	3,027	6[b]	28
1987	4,343	7[b]	4,701	8[b]	4,765	8[b]	31
1992	6,945	10[b]	4,077	6[b]	3,584	6[b]	34
1997	8,261	14[b]	5,100	10[b]	3,107	6[b]	43

a Formerly called Chippenham.

b In third place behind the Liberals.

Perhaps the best demonstration of the sheer perversity of our voting system can be found in the Newbury by-election itself. It was May 1993. The Labour Party was riding high in the polls. It had a 14-point lead over the Tories in the national opinion polls. It had made sweeping gains in the county council elections on the same day as the by-election. If it had been a general election, Labour would have won with an overall majority of more than 80 seats. Yet in Newbury its vote shrank to 1.99 per cent, the lowest vote that any Labour parliamentary candidate had won in any election or by-election since 1918.

A similar thing happened in the re-run Winchester election in November 1997. On the day of the election the Labour Party stood at 59 per cent in the polls, one of its highest poll leads in any month since the war. Local party activists worked valiantly to increase Labour's share of the vote from its modest 11 per cent score in the general election six months earlier. But what happened was the opposite. Labour's vote shrank from 11 per cent to 1.7 per cent as the Liberal Democrat regained the seat with a hugely increased majority. Labour's vote at 944 had fallen below 1,000 for the first time in living memory. Paradoxically, the reason why Labour did so badly in both Newbury and Winchester was the same as the reason why it was doing so well in the rest of the country. People were voting for, or had just voted for, a change of government. The way to express that desire in Newbury or Winchester was to vote for the Liberal Democrats. Labour's being at a record high in the national polls and a record low in Winchester were two sides of the same coin. They did so badly because they were doing so well.

Many Labour supporters were in the same dilemma elsewhere. In Richmond & Barnes, for instance, Labour supporters have long been in the situation of knowing it was a battle between the Tories and Liberal Democrats. At the 1987 election the Tories had 21,000 votes, the Liberals 20,000 and Labour 3,000. Thus in 1992 Labour voters knew that if they voted Liberal Democrat they might help to defeat the Tories. If they voted Labour they might, paradoxically, help the Tory to survive. The Labour candidate, Don Touhig, later to succeed Neil Kinnock as the MP for Islwyn in 1995, said only half jokingly to the Tory MP, Jeremy Hanley: "I'm the guy who's going to save you your seat." But it is the voting system that is the joke. FPTP means that a good Labour candidate can be the salvation of a Tory MP. It can mean, in an Alice-in-Wonderland way, that a vote for the Liberal Democrats can help Labour and a vote for Labour can help the Conservatives.

The Labour Party's voters often see this more clearly than the Labour Party itself. It was with the help of thousands of erstwhile Labour voters that the Liberal Democrats went on to win the newly named constituency, Richmond Park, in 1997. In other parts of the south, the shift was in the other direction. Many former tactical voters switched back to Labour, enabling it to recapture seats that it had not held since 1945, sometimes starting in third place and leapfrogging over the Liberal Democrats to win the seat from the Tories. For Labour voters it was often very difficult to know whether to persist with a tactical vote as the best way of securing Labour's return to power or whether to switch back to a Labour vote in the hope that enough other voters did so.

Labour's recapture of many of its traditional rural seats took people by surprise. They were astonished to see "Lab gain" flash up on their television screen next to such rural-sounding names as Forest of Dean, Kettering, North-west Leicestershire, North-west Norfolk, Scarborough & Whitby and Stroud. Some of these were seats that Labour used to hold in earlier decades thanks to the strength of the agricultural workers' union on the farms. It was always assumed that the party could not win those seats back because the farmworkers had left the land. But the truth was that the decline in the South and in rural England, although triggered by demographic factors, such as the migration of farm workers from the land, was held in place by the ratchet effect of tactical voting and third-party squeeze.

One of Tony Blair's great achievements was to break the ratchet and give people the confidence to vote Labour even in seats where Labour had been third at the last election. As a result, Labour won nine seats from third place and one from fourth. But there were other seats where Labour's vote hardly increased at all. It depended on the voters' perception of which party stood the better chance of defeating the Tory incumbent. This meant that non-Conservative voters were often desperate for information about how other people were intending to vote in their own constituencies. The rival Labour and Liberal Democrat candidates were of course keen to persuade people that they were in the best position to beat the Tories. But the voters had become wary of the parties' claims. They wanted objective information from an independent source. A campaign calling itself GROT (Get Rid Of the Tories) used local knowledge and psephologists to identify the party most likely to defeat the Conservatives in key marginals. But it was not until the *Observer* published the results of single-constituency polls in 16 marginal seats on the Sunday before the election that voters in those constituencies thought they were being told the truth.

The *Observer* did not poll those Labour target seats which by that stage of the election campaign were almost certain to fall into Labour's hands. Instead it picked out the kind of outside chances that no one seriously expected the Conservatives to lose but could theoretically change hands if the national opinion polls were right, such as Bristol West, Enfield Southgate, Hastings & Rye and St Albans. In 12 of the *Observer*'s 16 seats, the Conservatives lost. In all but one, Colchester, it was the party that emerged as the main challenger to the Conservatives that went on to win. In most cases the party that was ahead in the *Observer* poll strengthened its lead and the party that was trailing fell further behind. In Edinburgh Pentlands, for instance, Labour strengthened its leading position slightly and the SNP slipped further back into third place. In Taunton and Bridgwater in Somerset the second-place Liberal Democrats strengthened their vote and third-place Labour slipped back, although only in Taunton was it enough for the Liberal Democrats to take the seat.

In Enfield Southgate where Labour emerged as the only challenger to the Conservatives and only 4 points behind them, the poll almost certainly played a part in one of the most stunning results of election night, when Labour's Stephen Twigg took the seat from Michael Portillo. In Bristol West, Labour used the *Observer* poll to show the anti-Tory voters that its own polling was correct. In what was a three-way marginal, William Waldegrave would have survived. It was the *Observer* that won it for Labour. In Folkestone & Hythe Michael Howard was rather lucky because the poll showed his opponents were split evenly with the Liberal Democrats at 26 per cent and Labour at 25 per cent. The result was that the two non-Conservative candidates fought themselves to a stalemate and Michael Howard survived with only 39 per cent to the Liberal Democrats' 27 per cent and Labour's 26. Other beneficiaries of even splits between Liberal Democrat and Labour were Tom King in Bridgwater (37:34:25), David Prior in Norfolk North

TABLE 4.4 **% SUPPORT FOR PARTIES IN ICM *OBSERVER* POLL ON 27 APRIL 1997 COMPARED WITH 1992 AND 1997 ELECTIONS**

Constituency	*Party*	*1992*	*Poll*	*1997*
Bridgwater	Con	47	33	37
	Lib Dem	30	32	34
	Lab	22	30	25
Bristol West	Con	45	31	32
	Lab	23	39	35
	Lib Dem	29	24	28
Colchester	Con	42	32	31
	Lib Dem	33	31	34
	Lab	24	32	31
Edinburgh Pentlands	Con	40	34	32
	Lab	31	42	43
	SNP	16	15	13
Enfield Southgate	Con	58	45	41
	Lab	26	41	44
	Lib Dem	14	11	11
Folkestone & Hythe	Con	59	39	39
	Lib Dem	35	26	27
	Lab	12	25	25
Galloway & Upper Nithsdale	Con	42	29	31
	SNP	37	40	44
	Lab	13	23	16
Taunton	Con	46	39	39
	Lib Dem	41	38	43
	Lab	13	19	14

(37:34:25) and Tim Yeo in Suffolk South (37:28:29).

The *Mirror*, a supporter of electoral reform, ran tactical voting advice to its readers on Wednesday 30 April. In an article headlined "Get practical" it interviewed Labour voters voting tactically for the Liberal Democrats and vice versa. It asked its readers in the seats where only tactical voting could beat the Conservatives to show the article to their friends, neighbours and workmates.

It may appear to some that the FPTP system worked better in 1997 than in previous elections. After all the Labour Party was fairly well represented in the South-east again and it won a reasonable proportion of rural seats for the first time since 1945. But the system cured Labour under-representation in one region only by increasing the under-representation of other parties elsewhere. The level of under-representation in the Commons actually went up from 18 per cent in 1992 to 21 per cent in 1997. The Labour Party was over-represented by 21 per cent and the opposition parties shared the under-representation with Liberal Democrats 10, Conservatives 5 and others 6 per cent below their share of the votes.

These levels of over- or under-representation measure the exaggerative effect of the FPTP system or the deviation from proportionality (DV). In relation to their aggregate shares of the national vote the system has given Labour 21 per cent too many MPs and the opposition parties 21 per cent too few. By international standards that is a very high figure. Almost no other country has a voting system that creates such a high DV. But the national figure conceals much higher DV figures at regional level, for example 33 in Scotland, 32 in Yorkshire & Humberside and 32 in the North-west. The national DV is only as low as it is because the parties' over- and under-representation at regional level partly cancel one another out. As Patrick Dunleavy and Helen Margetts point out in *Britain Votes 1997*: "the British score for deviation from proportionality is misleadingly low if compared with other countries because areas of pro-Conservative deviation in the South-east are partly offset by areas of pro-Labour deviations in Scotland and the North". They point to the huge over-representation of the Conserva-

tives in the South-east in 1992, when they won 97 per cent of the seats
on 55 per cent of the vote, a regional DV of 43 per cent: "just about as
high as it is possible to get and still regard the political system as a liberal democracy".

TABLE 4.5   **OVER- AND UNDER-REPRESENTATION, 1997**

	Conservative			Labour			Lib Dem			DV
	votes	seats		votes	seats		votes	seats		
	%	%	%	%	%	%	%	%	%	%
South-east	42	65	+23	29	27	-2	23	8	-15	23
South-west	37	43	+6	26	29	+3	31	27	-4	9
London	31	15	-16	49	77	+28	15	8	-7	28
Eastern	40	59	+19	39	39	0	17	2	-15	20
E Midlands	35	32	-3	48	68	+20	14	0	-14	20
W Midlands	34	24	-10	48	75	+27	14	2	-12	27
Yorkshire	28	13	-15	52	84	+32	16	4	-12	32
North-west	27	10	-17	54	86	+32	14	3	-11	32
Northern	22	8	-14	61	89	+28	13	3	-10	28
Scotland	18	0	-18	46	78	+32	13	14	+1	33
Wales	20	0	-20	55	85	+30	12	5	-7	30
GB	31	26	-5	44	65	+21	17	7	-10	21
UK	31	25	-6	43	63	+20	17	7	-10	20

Figures from: Helen Margetts, Birkbeck College, London

Note: DV = deviation from proportionality

The result of tactical voting in the South and in rural areas is that
Labour's aggregate vote is artificially depressed by the third-party
squeeze. The same claim can also be made for the Liberal Democrats
or for the Greens, but that misses the point. It is Labour that is the
main challenger to the Conservatives for government and it is
Labour's national vote that is compared with the Conservatives'

national vote. On that basis Labour's vote was, in 1992, 7.5 per cent behind (34.4 per cent to 41.9 per cent in the United Kingdom, 35.2 per cent to 42.8 per cent in Great Britain). But this overstates the real gap between the parties. In the marginal seats where the voters had a real chance of defeating the Tories, they were far more likely to do so. The swings to Labour tended to be far higher.

Although the fraction of the country in which the battle is not Conservative-Labour has reduced slightly, it still applies to more than a quarter of the country where the Labour vote is artificially depressed by its greater exposure to third-party squeeze. The consolation is that the same phenomenon is now affecting the Conservatives. However, two wrongs do not make a right.

This raises the intriguing possibility that the opinion polls, far from being wrong at the 1992 election, were actually more accurate as a measure of the first preferences of the voters than the election itself. What they picked up until the eve of polling day was that more people wanted a Labour government than wanted a Conservative government. But the question that the pollsters ask, "If there were to be a general election tomorrow, which party would you vote for?", may elicit a different answer from some voters during an election campaign.

In normal times it is likely to be understood by most respondents as a general inquiry about which party they want to win the next election. In a campaign and especially in the days before polling day it is likely to be understood as a specific inquiry about which candidate they will end up voting for in the particular circumstances in their constituency. If there were a lot of voters who wanted to see a Conservative government replaced by a Labour government but realised that it would be futile to vote Labour in their own constituencies, then one would expect a shift away from Labour in the polls in the final days of the campaign, even as late as when the voter sees which parties are taking numbers outside the polling station. Women particularly were shown to make up their mind late. Pollsters have always used a different wording on the day before polling day, "In the general election tomorrow which party will you vote for?", and argue that this is just a technical change because the question is no longer hypothetical. But the answer may nevertheless change from a preference to a prediction for the many people who vote differently in hypothetical and real elections.

If this analysis is right, then much of the soul-searching and breast-beating that followed the 1992 election was based on a false premise. The pollsters were wrong to think they were totally wrong. Much of the explanation may lie in the meaning of their question changing for some voters as polling day approached. The Labour Party was also wrong to concentrate with such masochistic gloom on its 34.4 per cent share of the vote. To argue, as this book does, that the seats that each party wins ought to conform more closely to the proportion of votes each party wins is not the same thing as saying that people ought to pay more attention to the share of the vote that each party wins under the present system. On the contrary, reformers are well aware that the FPTP system distorts the result of elections. What they may not have appreciated so well in the past is that it can distort not only the shares of the seats allotted to each party but also their shares of the vote, because it distorts the behaviour of voters.

In the aftermath of the 1992 election pundits devoted thousands of words to ruminating on the "real" message that the voters had delivered. But the truth is that an electoral system sees the voter's mind through a glass darkly and we are not much wiser after the election about what the voters really "meant" or what policies they gave a "mandate" to. The pollsters who got it right in 1997 may still have a problem predicting a closer-run election as long as elections are fought using the current voting system.

The most common cliché used by politicians faced with the result of an opinion poll which they do not like is: "It's the real poll on election day that matters". The irony is that elections have become more and more like opinion polls and opinion polls have become more and more like elections should be. A general election reaches its result by sampling opinion in around 100 marginal seats just as an opinion poll takes a random sample of 103 constituencies. But an opinion poll does actually offer the voter a choice between all the parties, whereas in the real election the choice is restricted not only because it is impossible to vote for a party if it does not put up a candidate, but because it is futile to vote for a candidate who has no chance of winning. The opinion pollsters' response to this role reversal should be to learn to predict the irrationality of elections. The voters need to respond to it by insisting on a rational voting system.

5 POLARISATION

A glance at the constituency map after the 1945 election would have shown a chequerboard of red and blue squares across the whole country. Some of the constituencies that we now think of as typically Tory, or at a pinch Liberal, were Labour seats, including Cambridgeshire, Harborough, Sudbury, Taunton and Winchester. Other seats that we now think of as typical of the Labour inner cities were held by the Tories, including Liverpool East Toxteth and West Derby, Glasgow Central and Pollok.

Herbert Morrison acclaimed the election victory of 1945 as the point at which Labour became a truly national party. Indeed both main parties were as close to being national in 1945 as they have ever been. Support for both was spread fairly evenly across the country. In Scotland, where Labour is now so dominant, Labour held 37 seats and the Conservatives 29. Today Labour holds 56 and the Conservatives none. In the South Labour held even more seats than it does now. There were only three present-day counties, Surrey, Sussex and Dorset, where Labour was not represented.

But Labour's landslide victory in 1997 has failed to bring the party anywhere near the post-war peak. In the 1951 election, although Labour lost, it had a much higher general level of support throughout the country. There were only six seats in England where Labour failed to win at least a quarter of the vote. In 1997, the party's best election victory in its history, there were 101 seats where Labour failed to win a quarter of the vote. In 1951 Labour won more than 40 per cent of the vote in every seat in some rural counties such as Gloucestershire, Norfolk and Oxfordshire. In 1997 the figure was nowhere near that. It achieved 40 per cent of the vote in only one of the six seats in Oxfordshire and in only half the seats in Gloucestershire and Norfolk. That may owe something to the fact that Gloucestershire, Norfolk and Oxfordshire are among the poorer parts of the English countryside. But even in more affluent counties, such as Hampshire and Somerset, Labour achieved 30 per cent in every seat in 1951. In 1997 it reached 30 per cent in none of the present Somerset seats (although some of Somerset has been lost to Avon and its successor unitary authorities). In Surrey and Sussex Labour is doing much worse now than it did in the 1950s. Despite its striking victories on the south coast, winning the two Brighton seats, Hove and Hastings & Rye, Labour reached the 30 per cent level in less than one-quarter of the seats (six out of 27) compared with four-fifths (16 out of 20) in 1951.

TABLE 5.1   % SURREY LABOUR VOTE, 1951 AND 1997

	1951	1997	
Chertsey	39	21	Surrey Heath
	–	29	Runnymede & Weybridge
Dorking	34	15	Mole Valley
Epsom	31	24	Epsom & Ewell
Esher	29	23	Esher & Walton
Farnham	37	9	Surrey South West
Guildford	37	17	Guildford
Reigate	33	28	Reigate
Surrey East	27	21	Surrey East
Woking	31	21	Woking
	–	38	Spelthorne

But Labour overwhelmed the Tories in Scotland by 56 to nil. The Tories were practically obliterated in Glasgow. Their highest vote was 13 per cent and they were down to single figures in seven of the ten seats. They came third in seven seats and fourth in three. It is hard to believe that the Conservatives did better in Scotland in 1955 than Labour has ever done. They polled more than half the votes, an achievement Labour has never equalled. Since then they have lost two-thirds of their Scottish support and polled only 17.5 per cent in the

1997 election. There is a religious factor in this. Some of the Protestant working class used to vote Unionist and this is why Glasgow Govan remained Unionist, and therefore Conservative, until 1955 and Glasgow Scotstoun until 1959. But although the Conservative vote has fallen furthest in Govan, it has fallen almost as steeply in the rest of Glasgow.

TABLE 5.2 % GLASGOW CONSERVATIVE VOTE, 1951 AND 1997

	1951	1997
Cathcart	71	13
Central	40	–
Govan	50	9
Hillhead	65	–
Maryhill	36	6
Pollok	55	6
Shettleston	37	6
Springburn	38	6

Labour rediscovered some of its rural support in the 1997 election and some of the areas that had Labour representation in the late 1940s and 1950s went Labour again. Norfolk was once the home of a raw socialism preached by Methodist ministers and farmworkers' leaders. As well as the two Norwich MPs, five of the six rural Norfolk MPs were once Labour. The Forest of Dean in Gloucestershire was once a Labour stronghold with a majority of more than 30 per cent. North Kent was a Labour area until the 1970s with a Labour hall in every village. North Essex also boasted a rural Labour tradition. But Labour gradually lost its English rural seats. The last to go were Braintree in Essex and Faversham in North Kent in 1970, King's Lynn in Norfolk in 1974 and the Forest of Dean, then called Gloucestershire West, in 1983. By the late 1980s the Labour tradition appeared to have died out in all these rural areas. They became almost as strongly Conservative as the rest of the countryside. But the 1997 election was like an archaeological dig. It uncovered hidden layers of Labour support in rural areas with a Labour tradition. Labour won back Norfolk North West (the old King's Lynn), the Forest of Dean, Braintree and Harwich in Essex and a string of seats on the North Kent coast, including Chatham & Aylesford, Gillingham, Sittingbourne & Sheppey and Thanet South.

It will be an uphill task for the newly elected Labour MPs to hold these rural seats in future elections, and if they fail the Labour support in these areas may go back to sleep for another generation. Viability is the key to Labour's rural support. If it looks as if Labour can win, there will be many voters who rediscover their Labour roots. If the same happens in small towns, there may be enough Labour voters to win a council seat, but not enough to win a parliamentary seat. Council elections preserve pockets of Labour support in small towns such as Chipping Norton in Oxfordshire and Bridgwater in Somerset. As long as Labour continues winning elections in these areas, people will continue to vote Labour. Even one or two defeats does not necessarily mean that Labour voters will lose heart. But once a seat has been lost by a substantial margin, there comes a point at which Labour supporters give up hope of regaining it. Then the Labour vote falls sharply.

What has happened in the last 50 years is that the constituency map has lost its chequered look. Labour areas have become more Labour. Conservative areas have become more Conservative. The larger industrial areas and conurbations have turned into solid red blobs on the map while small towns and rural areas have turned into a sea of blue in between. Until the 1997 elections, most of Labour's support was concentrated in only six contiguous areas: Scotland's central belt, Tyne-Tees, Manchester-Merseyside-North Wales, the Midland conurbation, south Wales and London. 83 per cent of Labour seats are still in one of these six areas and 95 per cent adjoin at least one other Labour seat.

One can characterise this polarisation in three ways. It can be called a north-south polarisation, but that is perhaps the least accurate. Many parts of the north are strongly Tory. It is more accurate to call it an urban-rural polarisation. In cities such as Manchester, Liverpool and

Glasgow, the Conservatives held half the seats until 1955 (four of nine in Manchester, six of nine in Liverpool, seven of 14 in Glasgow), but now hold none. Cities such as Blackpool and Brighton were once Tory strongholds but are now held by Labour. Rural areas in England, even some in the north of England, have become more Tory.

TABLE 5.3   **POLARISATION OF LABOUR AND CONSERVATIVE SEATS, 1945–97**

	Seats in South[a]		Seats in Scotland	
	Lab	Con	Lab	Con
1945	53	75	37	29
1950	33	109	37	32
1951	25	118	35	35
1955	21	127	34	36
1959	13	131	38	31
1964	26	119	43	24
1966	38	105	46	20
1970	12	133	44	23
1974 Feb	21	136	40	21
1974 Oct	29	128	41	16
1979	13	146	44	22
1983	3	168	41	21
1987	3	169	50	10
1992	10	161	49	11
1997	59	109	56	0

a   South-east of England outside London, South-west and East Anglia.

The Conservatives won no MPs in Wales for the first time since 1906 and in Scotland for the first time ever. In their election book, David Butler and Dennis Kavanagh declared: "The 1997 election marked a reversal of the long-term trend towards the geographical polarisation between a Conservative south and Labour north". Ian McAllister also observes, in *Britain Votes 1997*, that: "The regional polarisation in the vote peaked in 1987." But was it a reversal, or perhaps just an easing or a hiatus in the trend? Compared with the late 1940s or 1950s, the country is still much more politically polarised than it was. And it is only an approximation to say that it is polarised between south and north or between rural and urban. The most accurate description is that it is a polarisation into areas where each party is predominant. Predominantly Labour areas become more Labour and predominantly Tory areas more Tory.

The FPTP voting system does not cause this regional cleavage, but it exaggerates it. In predominantly Tory areas in the south Labour supporters often saw no point in voting for candidates who had no chance of success. They switched to the Liberals. That gave more prominence to the Liberals. Labour fell to third place and lost credibility. Even more people then abandoned the Labour Party. When national Labour politicians were interviewed on radio or TV, they were MPs for other parts of the country speaking in the accents of other regions. In the 1980s voters in these areas had ceased to think of Labour, at least nationally, as a party that spoke their language or that articulated their concerns. The same thing happened to the Tories in parts of Scotland. They fell into third place behind the SNP. When national Tory politicians appeared on TV, they were almost always English and that undermined the credibility of the Scottish Tories further, thus reinforcing the trend which culminated in the wipe-out of Conservative Scottish representation in the Commons in May 1997.

This polarisation reached into every part of the body politic, including the political parties themselves. Labour's policy-making and communications suffered because the Labour Party was polarised along similar lines to Britain as a whole. Party decision-makers, shadow cabinets and Labour prime ministers almost all come from safe seats in Scotland, Wales and English cities. The party may try to compensate for this, but the positions of power are usually held by MPs representing safe seats and they may also see issues through the prism of their constituents' interests. Policy will inevitably be skewed towards the interests of the regions where the party is strong. That can be seen clearly in the case of the Conservatives in Scotland, but it is equally true, or – perhaps more importantly – seen to be true, in the case of Labour and the south. That perception reinforces the process of political polarisation.

If the Conservative government of the 1980s created a country of two nations, of north and south, of rich and poor, of winners and losers, then the electoral system was its midwife. FPTP encourages the emergence of a dominant party in constituencies, in regions, because it recognises only majorities, or more correctly winners, and ignores minorities.

The majority feel encouraged because their votes have been effective and they have an MP. The minority may be spurred to greater efforts to win the next time, but if they are defeated too often and by too wide a margin, they may feel unrepresented in parliament and alienated and discouraged.

At the constituency level this produces an incumbency factor. People vote for sitting MPs because they are good MPs or have done them a favour or simply because they are the MPs. Psephologists argue about how much the incumbency factor is worth. The most recent calculations put it at around 1,500 votes. That is of course an average, and individual MPs or candidates may make much more difference than that. But the point is that the incumbency factor is now about twice as high as it used to be.

The same factor exists at the regional level. If one party is dominant in a region, then its politicians will appear more often in the local press and on regional television. The dominant party will have more politicians to choose from and because it has more safe seats it will have more experienced politicians. In the Southern ITV area, for instance, before the 1997 election, programme producers could choose between more than 50 Tory MPs and only one Labour MP. In the North-east, Conservative MPs are a rare species and any Tory MP who represents a seat in the region is unlikely to be senior in the party hierarchy. Thus the dominant party in a region is likely to have long-standing well-known politicians sitting in safe seats and the minority party is likely to have little-known MPs sitting in marginal seats. In this way the dominant party becomes even more dominant.

If you draw a line from the Severn to the Wash, there are two Englands of roughly the same size that seem politically quite different. Before 1997, the Conservatives have three-quarters of their seats in the South and only one-quarter in the North. Labour was the mirror image. It had two-thirds of its English seats north of the Severn-Wash line and only one-third south of that. The cabinet and the shadow cabinet display an even stronger bias. In the cabinet 50 per cent represent English constituencies in the North or the Midlands and only 15 per cent represent the South. In the shadow cabinet, two-thirds represent the South and one-third represent the Midlands or the North.

But these stark contrasts represent a truth about the electoral system rather than a truth about the country. Even in 1992 Labour's vote was far more evenly spread than such figures suggest. Labour had more voters in the South-east region (outside London) than it had in the whole of Scotland. Yet it had three MPs in the South-east and 49 in Scotland. Labour had more votes in the home counties around London (Surrey, Sussex, Kent, Essex, Hertfordshire, Buckinghamshire and

TABLE 5.4   LABOUR VOTES AND SEATS, 1992 AND 1997

	1992		*1997*	
	Votes	*Seats*	*Votes*	*Seats*
South-east[a]	1,338,297	3	1,840,917	36
South-west	561,847	4	734,381	15
Yorkshire	1,266,810	34	1,339,578	47
Scotland	1,142,866	49	1,283,353	56
Northern	914,712	29	991,697	32
Wales	865,633	27	885,935	34

a South-east includes Beds, Essex and Herts, which are now in Eastern.

Berkshire) than it had in Wales. Yet it had only one MP in the home counties and 27 in Wales.

In 1992 the South-east was Labour's second biggest region in terms of votes. More votes were cast for Labour in the South-east than in Yorkshire, the North-east or Scotland. Yet in terms of seats it was the worst region for the Labour Party with only three seats, Southampton Itchen, Oxford East and Thurrock. In 1997 Labour increased its representation but still had only 36 MPs in the South-east and 56 in Scotland. The 1997 result was so bad for the Conservatives throughout the country that these patterns are hidden, but they may emerge in local and European elections.

The voting system can be compared with a hall of reflecting mirrors. It makes those of less than average height look like dwarfs and those of more than average height look like giants. Yet it has one extraordinary quality that no hall of mirrors possesses. It tends to make people become more like their reflections. Through the process of polarisation it makes the tall become taller and the small become smaller. And as they become taller and smaller, their images become even taller and even smaller.

It is through the grotesque distortion of the hall of mirrors that our political perceptions are formed. Northerners have thought of the south of England as being typically Tory and posh. Southerners think of the North, and indeed central Scotland and south Wales, as being typically Labour and working-class. The electoral system encourages people to think that these gross generalisations are true. Yet it has also had the effect, in terms of voting rather than class, of making the perception become more true.

6 DEMORALISATION

Ever since the psephologist Robert McKenzie demonstrated his swingometer on television, voters have understood that the outcome of an election depends on the result in a relatively small number of marginal seats. If they are voters in Tunbridge Wells or Tottenham, they know there is little they can do as individuals to change the outcome of the election, but if they are voters in Southampton Test or Bolton West, they could well hold the fate of the nation in their hands.

TABLE 6.1   CONSERVATIVE-LABOUR MARGINAL
             SEATS, 1955–97

	Number	Total seats	%
1955	166	630	27
1959	157	630	26
1964	166	630	27
1966	155	630	26
1970	149	630	25
1974 Feb	119	635	20
1974 Oct	98	635	16
1979	108	635	18
1983	80	650	13
1987	87	650	14
1992	97	651	15
1997	114	659	17

What is perhaps less well understood is that the functioning of the voting system depends on having a relatively large number of marginal seats. A study in 1950 by two academics, Kendall and Stuart, showed that the system worked in the normal way, by which a fairly small shift in votes produced a big turnaround in seats, only as long as three constituencies in ten were marginals. If the number dropped below that, the system would become less responsive.

As Table 6.1 on the previous page shows, the number of Conservative-Labour marginals has fallen significantly over the last 40 years. There has been an increase in the number of Conservative-Liberal or Conservative-nationalist marginals, but that does nothing to make the system responsive to a swing between the two main parties.

The word marginal is used in this table to mean the seats that each of the main parties would have to win to win power. In an election that resulted in a dead heat, they would be the seats where Labour or Conservative had a majority that amounted to less than 10 per cent of their combined vote (the tinted bars in Figure 6.1 on page 54). In the 1950s and 1960s almost every third seat was a marginal, but now it is only every sixth or seventh seat.

This can be seen better on Figure 6.1 which shows the seats ranged according to the size of the Labour or Conservative majority as a proportion of the Labour-Conservative vote. The middle of each histogram represents the marginals and the left and right represent the safe seats. In 1955 the marginals form a single point in the centre of the histogram which slopes sharply as it moves down towards the safe seats. By 1979 the situation has changed and there are twin points, one representing Tory seats with a majority of 30–40 per cent and the other representing Labour seats with a majority of 20–30 per cent. By 1992 it has changed again and the shape is more rectangular, representing an even spread between safe and marginal seats.

The single point in 1955 represents the distinctive feature of the FPTP system, known to psephologists as the cube law. What this law means in effect is that a winning party will win an extra 3 per cent of the seats for every extra 1 per cent of the vote. If it wins by 51 to 49 per cent of the votes, the seats will be divided 53:47. If it wins by 53 to 47 per cent of the votes, the seats will be divided 59:41. This exaggerative effect is seen as a benefit by supporters of the FPTP system. It exaggerates the lead of the first party over the second party, so that

FIGURE 6.1 THE FALLING NUMBER OF MARGINALS
No. constituencies by size of majority (% Lab/Con vote)

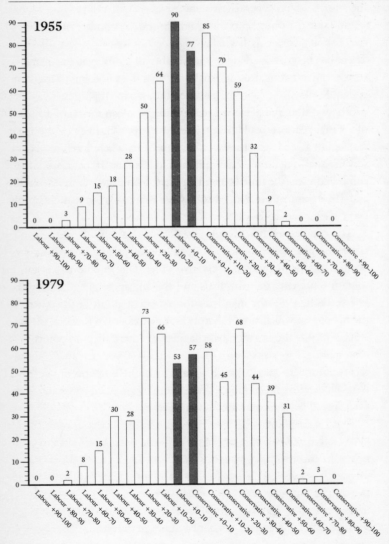

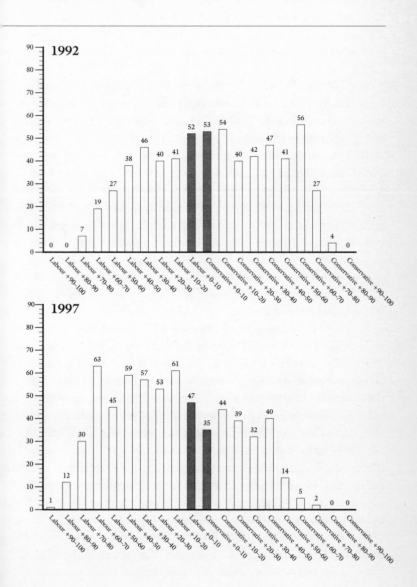

even a narrow lead in votes will give a party a comfortable majority in seats and a comfortable majority in votes will give it a landslide. This winner's bonus is supposed to be the system's way of avoiding hung parliaments or weak governments with precarious majorities. But the cube law is not a law of mathematics or a law of the electoral system. It is simply an observation of the way that the electoral system has worked in the past. It is a law only in the sense of being – or once having been – a useful guide to predicting how many seats a party will win on a given share of the vote.

What has happened over the last three elections, as John Curtice and Michael Steed have shown, is that the cube law became very much weaker in 1987 and almost disappeared in 1992, although it recovered some of its force in 1997. Some argued mistakenly that the system was proportional to the top two parties if the other parties were ignored. John Major had almost no winner's bonus over Labour. Tony Blair recovered some of the winner's bonus in 1997 but as Curtice and Steed commented in their appendix to Butler and Kavanagh's election book: "The electoral system is still a long way from providing the kind of winner's bonus that the system regularly provided until 1974."

Supporters of FPTP have long defended it on the grounds that it delivers stable and secure government by exaggerating the lead of the largest party over the opposition. But this supposed benefit is not a function of the system but accidental and unpredictable. Its other supposed benefit is that it discriminates against small parties, but in fact it over-represents the small parties whose support is geographically concentrated such as the Ulster Unionists, the Democratic Unionists and the Welsh nationalist party, Plaid Cymru. As a result there are more parties represented in our parliament than there are in most European parliaments elected by proportional representation. We have nine parties elected to the Westminster Parliament and even the Dutch with their fairly pure proportional system have no more.

The more serious malfunction of the system is the decline in the number of Conservative-Labour marginals. This means that fewer and fewer voters feel that their vote can make any practical difference or that their vote gives them any purchase on the choice of government. Of course it is only as long as the strongholds continue to vote Labour that the marginals are in a position to put Labour in power, so that voters in Labour strongholds do have a say. If they stopped voting Labour collectively, Labour would be sunk. But individually their votes would make no difference. And with fewer than 100 Conservative-Labour marginals among the 659 constituencies, it means that 85 per cent of the electorate, or 37 million people, live in constituencies where their vote is unlikely to make any difference and where in consequence the parties are unlikely to make much of an effort. There is less incentive for voters to vote and less pressure on them to do so. There is less point in local parties knocking on doors and people putting up posters. This demarginalisation of constituencies leads inevitably to demotivation among voters and demoralisation among party activists.

TABLE 6.2   % NON-VOTERS, 1955–97

	Safe seats	Marginal seats	Difference (% points)
1955	26	21	+5
1970	31	27	+4
1979	25	23	+2
1992	24	21	+3
1997	29 (33[a])	26 (26[a])	+3 (+7[a])

a Labour only.

Table 6.2 shows that abstention has always been greater in safe seats than in marginal seats; in 1955 the figures were 26 and 21 per cent, in the last election 29 and 26 per cent. On this basis in the 1997 election there were probably more than 750,000 abstainers in safe seats, who did not bother to vote because the seat was safe and would have voted if they had been living in a marginal seat. Non-voters in safe Labour seats rose to 33 per cent of the electorate whereas in marginal seats the figure was 26 per cent.

TABLE 6.3   HIGHEST TURNOUTS, 1992 AND 1997

	1992				1997		
Constituency	Turnout %	1987 Majority %	Winning party	Constituency	Turnout %	1992 Majority %	Winning party
NW Leicestershire	86.1	13.4	Con	Mid Ulster	86.1	18.0	Sinn Fein
Monmouth	86.1	19.9	Con	Brecon & Radnorshire	82.2	0.3	Lib Dem
Brecon & Radnor	85.9	0.1	Con	Stirling	81.8	1.5	Lab
Ribble Valley[a]	85.7	39.4	Con	Wirral South[c]	81.0	22.2	Lab
Mid-Staffordshire[b]	85.7	25.9	Con	Monmouth	80.8	6.3	Lab
South Derbyshire	85.5	15.9	Con	Ayr	80.2	0.2	Lab
Sherwood	85.5	7.7	Lab	Vale of Glamorgan	80.0	0.0	Lab
Richmond & Barnes	85.0	3.9	Con	Leicestershire NW	79.8	1.6	Lab
West Derbyshire	85.0	17.9	Con	Cardiff North	79.7	6.2	Lab
Hazel Grove	84.9	3.4	Con	Galloway & Upper Nithsdale	79.7	5.5	SNP

a 1991 by-election – Lib Dem majority 10.0%.
b 1990 by-election – Lab majority 16.8%.
c 1997 by-election – Lab majority 18.2%.

Turnout is influenced by a number of other factors including the length of the campaign, the level of interest, the stability of the electorate, the socioeconomic class of the voter, even the weather. The marginality of seats should be only a small factor. But in fact, as Table 6.3 opposite shows, there is a very significant correlation between high turnout and marginality. This may be because people feel their vote is more likely to count in a marginal and are therefore more strongly motivated to cast their vote. It may be because the political parties are working harder at persuading their supporters to vote in marginal seats. It may be because there is more media and voter interest where the result hangs in the balance than in a safe seat. In practice it is impossible to disentangle these three reasons.

In 1997 the Vale of Glamorgan was the most marginal seat in the country, held by the Conservatives in 1992 by a majority of 19. Brecon & Radnorshire was the seat at the top of the Liberal Democrats' target list with a Conservative majority of only 130. Galloway & Upper Nithsdale was at the top of the SNP's target list. Ayr was the most marginal Conservative seat in Scotland, held by the Conservatives by 85 votes. Stirling and Leicestershire North-West were both on the list of the Conservative super-marginals held by a majority in three figures. Cardiff North was another seat on Labour's target list. There seems to be a correlation as well between high turnout and seats which have recently changed hands in high profile by-elections. The drama of the by-election appears to add to voters' interest in the ensuing general election. That is certainly true of Wirral South, which the Conservatives had held by a comfortable majority of 16 per cent in 1992 and which would not have been considered marginal in the 1997 election if it had not been won by Labour in a by-election in March 1997. Vale of Glamorgan and Monmouth also witnessed dramatic by-elections in 1989 and 1991 and Brecon & Radnorshire was the scene of another famous by-election in 1985. They were all regained by the Conservatives in 1992 but won back by the by-election victors in 1997.

What is clear from Table 6.4 on the following page is that low turnout is overwhelmingly a problem of inner city seats. This is partly

TABLE 6.4   LOWEST TURNOUTS, 1992 AND 1997

1992				1997			
Constituency	*Turnout* %	*1987 Majority* %	*Winning party*	*Constituency*	*Turnout* %	*1992 Majority* %	*Winning party*
Peckham	53.9	28.8	Lab	Liverpool Riverside	51.9	64.4	Lab
Liverpool Riverside	54.6	59.4	Lab	Hackney North & Stoke Newington	52.2	30.9	Lab
Newham North-West	56.0	30.0	Lab	Manchester Central	52.6	56.2	Lab
Sheffield Central	56.1	50.6	Lab	Sheffield Central	53.0	52.2	Lab
Manchester Central	56.9	49.4	Lab	Birmingham Ladywood	54.2	40.7	Lab
Newham South	60.2	9.3	Lab	West Bromwich West	54.4	19.3	Lab (Speaker)
Newham North-East	60.3	21.1	Lab	Leeds Central	54.7	39.5	Lab
Manchester Gorton	60.8	31.1	Lab	Hackney S & Shoreditch	54.7	24.4	Lab
Leeds Central	61.3	30.1	Lab	Kensington & Chelsea	54.7	11.5	Con
East Antrim	62.5	45.9	UU	Vauxhall	55.5	26.9	Lab

because of the high housing mobility in these areas. According to the 1991 census, 22 per cent of the electorate of Kensington & Chelsea had been at a different address a year earlier. But it is also because of the low incentive to vote in seats where the result is a foregone conclusion. In the case of Kensington & Chelsea there must be many electors double-registered who can choose where to cast their vote. The same is true of students in many city centre seats. A third reason will be the high proportion of typically low turnout groups in these seats, especially young voters and some categories of ethnic minority voters.

It is difficult to say how much of this differential turnout is because voters are keener in marginal seats and how much because parties put greater pressure on them to vote. A study after the 1992 election by David Denver and Gordon Hands of Lancaster University measured the extent to which parties concentrate their resources on marginal seats. It found that all local political parties put roughly the same effort into basic services to the voters, such as delivery of election addresses and doorstep visits by candidates, whether they were fighting safe, marginal or hopeless seats. But when it came to putting up posters, delivering leaflets and canvassing, Labour and the Liberal Democrats concentrated their resources on marginal seats and the Conservatives tended to put more effort into their safe seats. When it came to knocking up voters on polling day, all parties concentrated on marginal seats, but Labour more so than the others.

TABLE 6.5 MEMBERSHIP ELECTIONEERING NUMBERS, 1992

Seat	Members			Campaign workers			Polling day workers		
	Con	Lab	L/D	Con	Lab	L/D	Con	Lab	L/D
Safe	2,401	521	252	140	48	53	402	118	133
Marginal	1,215	553	377	84	81	92	240	205	190
Weak	315	362	141	16	35	23	36	84	49

TABLE 6.6   ELECTIONEERING ACTIVITIES, 1992

Seat	Leaflets delivered			Posters displayed			% canvassed		
	Con	Lab	L/D	Con	Lab	L/D	Con	Lab	L/D
Safe	70	61	47	1,909	2,610	1,790	51	32	25
Marginal	73	128	130	1,648	4,691	3,278	45	57	27
Weak	34	68	44	928	2,027	872	23	24	11

TABLE 6.7   ELECTIONEERING RESOURCES, 1992

Seat	Computers used			Election addresses[a]			Candidates' visits[a]		
	Con	Lab	L/D	Con	Lab	L/D	Con	Lab	L/D
Safe	1.4	1.6	1.0	4.8	4.7	5.0	4.1	3.0	2.6
Marginal	1.5	3.9	2.9	4.7	4.6	4.7	4.1	3.4	3.1
Weak	0.5	1.6	1.5	4.8	4.6	4.4	3.7	3.3	2.6

a Agents' estimates of effort on scale from 1 to 5.

It is clear from the three tables above that the Labour Party, although it discourages voters even in the most hopeless seats from engaging in tactical voting to try to beat the system, indulges in a great deal of tactical resourcing. To a greater extent than the Tories and even sometimes the Liberal Democrats, it directs its workers and its resources away from safe or hopeless seats and towards marginals. The Tories have either never sought or never achieved this tactical direction of resources and in seven of the nine categories in the above tables they put more effort into safe seats than marginals.

The explanation may lie in the deployment of Conservative agents. Labour tends to concentrate its full-time agents, wherever possible, in marginal seats. The Conservatives have many more full-time agents but they work in safe seats as well as marginals. Their main job is to raise funds by building up membership in constituency associations and that is much easier to do in safe seats. As a result the bulk of the Tory members are in safe seats and it is not always easy to persuade them to go and help in faraway marginals.

It is also possible that Tory safe seats are much more vulnerable to a Liberal Democrat attack than safe Labour seats, so the Tories need to keep an army of helpers on stand-by in every seat. So many Tory strongholds have fallen to a surprise Liberal assault in a by-election that they can never afford to relax. In Tory safe seats the enemy is the Liberals. In Labour safe seats the enemy is complacency. Labour redeploys its agents away from safe seats to marginals with apparent impunity, but in the long term this affects Labour voters and Labour party members in both safe and hopeless seats. In safe seats the Labour voters become disillusioned, passive, used to seeing Labour only at election times, if then, and Labour's majority and Labour's membership are eroded. Labour party members become accustomed to winning elections with very little effort and it is inevitable that winning too easily will lead some to complacency, some to arrogance, some even to corruption.

In seats where Labour is not thought to have a real chance Labour supporters have escaped from the futility of voting Labour by voting tactically. Keeping up the morale of Labour Party members in a constituency where there is not thought to be any possibility of winning is very difficult. In some areas Labour can still win council or European elections even if it cannot win parliamentary elections and this gives the local party a continuing purpose. But in other areas they are totally removed from power or the possibility of power. The constituency parties can become intellectual debating societies where even members who put Labour posters in their windows may vote tactically. In some areas they gradually lose members, leaving a hard core who have little contact with Labour voters or grasp of the policies needed to attract them. Many of them do not even support the reform of the voting system which is the real author of their misfortunes.

7 DOMINATION

In the 1950s and 1960s people talked about a two-party system. In the 1970s they talked about a three-party system. In the 1980s they began to talk of a one-party system. That turned out to be an inaccurate description. But there are very few who would still subscribe to the pendulum theory of politics that Labour and Conservatives will naturally take it in turns to hold office.

In the early 1990s it began to look as though the pendulum had stuck. The result was a violent swing back in 1997. But there is no reason to believe that there will be anything either smooth or regular about future changes of government. Quite apart from the unpredictability of public opinion, the FPTP voting system is erratic and unpredictable in its consequences.

TABLE 7.1 **PARTIES IN GOVERNMENT, 1919–1997**

	Con		Lab		Lib	
	Years	Months	Years	Months	Years	Months
Ministers in govt	57	1	26	6	9	1
	72%		33%		11%	
Majority govt	48	8	14	2	0	0
	62%		18%		0%	
Secure majority	48	6	9	10	0	0
	61%		12%		0%	

Even if Labour is at the start of a long period in office, it remains true that the Conservatives have been in power for four times as long as Labour in the period since the end of the first world war. From 1918, when Labour started fighting elections on something approach-

ing a national basis, till the beginning of 1998, the Conservatives have
been in power with a majority for 48 years, Labour for 14; the Conservatives for three years out of every five, Labour for barely one year
out of every six; the Conservatives have won elections with double-
figure majorities on 11 occasions, Labour only three times – in 1945,
1966 and 1997. Yet the difference in the average Conservative and average Labour vote in the 21 elections since 1919 (excluding 1931
when the party system broke down) is not very large: 42.6 per cent for
the Conservatives and 39.3 per cent for Labour.

James McCormick expressed it clearly in the *Scotsman* on 19 July
1995: "Across all general elections since 1945, the Conservatives have
spent 66 out of every 100 months in majority government, while
Labour has held office on its own for 32 of them. Yet, the share of
votes cast for each party (out of 400 million votes in total) tells a very
different story. Far from outpolling Labour by two to one, the Tories
won 45 votes in every hundred to Labour's 42."

It made some sense to talk about the swing of the pendulum in
the years between 1945 and 1979 when the Conservative and Labour
parties were each in power for 17 years. But to liken it to the swing
of a pendulum is to suggest that the opposition's return to power is
regular and inevitable. Even during the immediate post-war period it
was never regular and it was certainly not inevitable. Labour had lost
three elections and almost given up any hope of winning when a
series of government scandals and a change of prime minister helped
Harold Wilson to scrape in by four seats in 1964. Labour was uni-
versally expected to lose when Ted Heath called a snap election in the
middle of a miners' strike in February 1974. Indeed the Tories out-
polled Labour by 11,872,180 to 11,645,616. But a quirk of the voting system gave Labour four more seats than the Tories and Labour
came back to office.

Both victories owed a good deal to luck. The idea that a Labour victory was or is inevitable should be compared not with a law of physics
which says that a pendulum that has lost its kinetic energy must swing
back but with the blind faith of a gambler who sits through a run of

losses believing their luck must return. There are two ways in which the
British electoral system is like a casino where the dice are loaded. There
is one bias that works in favour of the Conservatives and another bias
that usually works in Labour's favour. It is worth examining each in turn.

The first has to do with the geographical distribution of votes. To
do well in a FPTP system a party needs to have a vote that is neither too
concentrated nor too evenly spread. If it is too concentrated, the party
will be under-represented because so much of its support is piled up in
unnecessarily huge majorities. If it is too evenly spread, it risks not
being represented at all. What it needs is to have its supporters neither
too thickly nor too thinly spread, concentrated but not too concentrated, around the whole country.

TABLE 7.2   **LARGEST PERCENTAGE MAJORITIES,
1992 AND 1997**

1992			*1997*		
Constituency	*%*	*Winning party*	*Constituency*	*%*	*Winning party*
1. Blaenau Gwent	69.2	Lab	1. Bootle	74.4	Lab
2. Liverpool Riverside	64.4	Lab	2. Easington	71.6	Lab
3. Knowsley North	63.1	Lab	3. Blaenau Gwent	70.7	Lab
4. Barnsley East	63.0	Lab	4. Merthyr Tydfil	69.2	Lab
5. Rhondda	62.7	Lab	5. Liverpool Walton	67.2	Lab
6. Merthyr Tydfill	60.3	Lab	6. Barnsley Central	67.2	Lab
7. Liverpool Walton	59.9	Lab	7. Swansea East	66.1	Lab
8. Islwyn	59.4	Lab	8. Islwyn	65.7	Lab
9. Bootle	58.6	Lab	9. Tyne Bridge	65.7	Lab
24. Huntingdon	49.3	Con	198. Huntingdon	31.8	Con

One can construct a theoretical model to demonstrate this. The
Blue Party holds all its seats by majorities of 60:40 and the Red Party

holds its seats by majorities of 80:20. When the votes are totalled the Red Party has 600 and the Blue Party has 500, but the Blue Party has seven seats and the Red Party has four. This was how Labour lost the 1951 election despite having more votes than the Conservatives. Labour had millions of votes piled up in huge majorities in its strongholds. In some constituencies it had over 85 per cent of the vote. The Conservatives had their vote more efficiently spread. That still happens today. In 1997 the biggest majorities were all Labour.

This bias is sometimes cancelled out by another bias that works in Labour's favour. Because Labour represents the areas where the population is declining and because the constituency boundaries have hitherto been revised only every 15 years, Labour ends up with smaller constituencies towards the end of the cycle and it therefore needs fewer votes to win its seats. But this bias will be considerably reduced when the boundary commission completes its review. The boundary commission cannot of course correct the bias that geography confers on the Conservatives, so it ends up merely reinstating the pro-Tory bias in the system. The nature of the traditional Labour vote has been that it often concentrated in small pockets where most people vote Labour, whether a mining community, a shipbuilding town, the inner part of a city, a new town or, at a smaller level, a council housing estate, whereas Conservative voters have had fewer reasons to herd themselves together. The only artificial concentrations of Tory voters are fashionable areas at the centre of large cities, such as Chelsea, retirement resorts for the wealthy, such as Worthing and Eastbourne, and wealthy commuter areas where high house prices exclude all but the very rich, such as Esher or Knutsford. But Labour voters are far more concentrated in a Welsh valley or an inner city council estate than are Tory voters in a wealthy stockbroker belt.

The problem for Labour has been the large areas of the country where the Tory vote tends to be 45–55 per cent and Labour's support, while significant, will only exceed 35–45 per cent in an exceptional election. This tends to be true of most small towns and cities with populations of less than 100,000 and most suburban areas. These areas may have a fair amount of industry, a fair number of industrial workers and an average proportion of council tenants, but not in sufficient numbers to elect a Labour MP in a normal year. The danger for the Labour Party is that in due course Labour voters will give up hope of electing their own MP and the process of polarisation will set in.

Labour was fortunate in the 1997 election in that the distribution of its vote, which is usually a disadvantage, turned into an advantage. In the seats where it had traditionally won 30–40 per cent of the vote, the Conservative vote collapsed and Labour won. Like all systematic biases it must reverse itself on the scale and Labour had passed that point. As Ron Johnston and others comment in *Anatomy of a Labour Landslide*: "Parties differ in the efficiency of their vote distributions. Labour has traditionally suffered because of this. It has tended to win by large majorities in its areas of strength and so gained fewer seats than might have been the case if its support was more evenly spread across the country. In 12 of the 13 previous elections this benefited the Conservatives. In 1997 it benefited Labour."

But will Labour's good fortune last? In theory the polarisation of the country into Labour and Conservative halves need not favour either party, but in practice it tends to lock Labour into the parts of the country where the population is falling, like the old industrial areas and the inner cities, and undermines its support in the areas where the population has been increasing over the last 20 years, the countryside, the south-east, the south-west and the new industrial areas.

In this respect the tacticalisation of the vote can be a one-way street for Labour. In the areas in the south which are becoming more industrial, often with new industries, where problems of unemployment, lack of training and poverty are beginning to be recognised, and the protection of public services is becoming an important issue, the Labour Party may still be struggling to find its natural voters. The same is true of areas which have been hopeless for Labour for many years until a boundary change makes them theoretically winnable for Labour again. If tactical voting has taken a hold, it may be difficult for Labour to persuade people that Labour now has a chance. That is one reason why boundary reviews can be so damaging: Labour loses seats in its traditional areas where the population is falling but finds it more difficult to pick up new seats in newly industrialised areas where the population is rising. Labour's success in 1997 in winning seats like Milton Keynes and Crawley, seats which in many respects ought to have gone Labour some time ago in the sense that most of the voters voted Labour in the constituencies they lived in before, may well have broken the jinx for Labour.

The danger facing the Labour Party until the 1997 election was not that it might not have been polarised into half the country but into less than half. It had gained the votes of many middle-class Scots but it had lost the votes of many working-class Southerners and it was not a fair exchange. There were far fewer middle-class Scots than working-class Southerners. There are few remaining seats that Labour can realistically win in Scotland.

The result of the 1997 election represents an important breakthrough for the Labour Party. It has not only restored its own confidence in its ability to win seats in the South, in East Anglia, in semi-rural areas and in the more prosperous outer suburbs of the great cities; it has also made important advances in the new industrial centres, the M4 corridor and the home counties.

But it has not won this victory because the biases in the system have disappeared. On the contrary, the biases just happen to have worked in its favour in one election. It remains to be seen who will be favoured by the system's biases next time round if the system remains. The fact that biases can work in both directions does not mean it would not be better to have a system without biases. As Curtice and Steed commented on the election: "There was no electoral recovery for the two-party system. The first-past-the-post electoral system worked even more perversely than usually."

8 DICHOTOMY

In the second half of the 19th century Britain was a two-party system and the Whigs and Tories alternated in power. It was reasonable for Bagehot to feel that, even if his Whig vote was wasted in an agricultural county, it was balanced by Whig votes in industrial counties. It was also reasonable for him to feel confident that, if the Whigs were trounced in one election, they might well be triumphant in the next. The principle of swings and roundabouts meant that neither party felt nationally disadvantaged. And the swing of the pendulum meant that neither party felt perpetually excluded from power.

TABLE 8.1 **TOP TWO PARTIES: NUMBER OF CONSTITUENCIES, 1992 AND 1997[a]**

Parties	1992	1997
Con & Lab	409	432
Con & Lib Dem	164	112
Lab & SNP	32	43
Lab & Lib Dem	12	36
Con & SNP	6	6
Con & Plaid Cymru	3	–
Lab & Plaid Cymru	2	8
Lab & Other	3	1
Lib Dem & SNP	–	1

a Excluding Northern Ireland, Tatton and the Speaker's seat.

The mistaken assumption made by nearly everyone interested in politics until the 1960s, that is not only politicians, but political scientists and members of political parties, was that a voting system that encourages a contest between two parties will always encourage a contest between the same two parties. Clearly it has not. Of the 641 constituencies in Britain only two-thirds are Conservative-Labour battles. In 112 seats the battle is between Conservative and Liberal Democrats. In two-thirds of the seats in Scotland the battle is between the SNP and either Labour or Conservatives. In about a fifth of the seats in Wales the battle is with Plaid Cymru. The only kind of battle that is relatively uncommon is between Labour and the Liberal Democrats. That is found in only 37 seats in the whole country – around one in 20.

In every constituency politics tends to polarise into a battle between the incumbent and a main challenger. There are parts of the country where the electoral battle is blue-red, parts where it is blue-yellow, parts where it is orange-green. There are very few areas where it is red-yellow, although there are many areas where the main political battle is between red and yellow to be the main challenger.

The legacy of the 1983 and 1987 elections was to leave a number of seats where Labour and the Liberal Democrats were vying for second place behind the Conservatives. In Mid-Staffordshire, for instance, both parties were a long way behind the Tories in the ratio 50:25:25. But in Cambridge they were both within striking distance of the Tories, roughly in the ratio of 40:30:30. In both of those seats Labour won, taking Mid-Staffordshire in a by-election in 1990, although it lost it again at the 1992 general election, and winning Cambridge at the 1992 general election, even though it started in third place. But it is a measure of the difficulties of winning from third place that Labour succeeded in doing it in only two seats in 1992, Cambridge and Plymouth Devonport. In 1997 it did so in ten seats: Aberdeen South, Bristol West, Conwy, Falmouth & Camborne, Hastings & Rye, Leeds North West, St Albans, Shrewsbury & Atcham, Sittingbourne & Sheppey and (from notional fourth place) Inverness East and Nairn & Lochaber.

Because of all these local variations it now makes much less sense to think of a general election as a single national battle between two parties. It is better to look at it as 659 constituency battles, each one different from its neighbours. How people will vote depends not only on which party they prefer in an ideal world but also on the chances of each candidate, the effort made by the parties and the encouragement given to voters to vote on tactical grounds. Psephologists try to measure the increase or decrease in tactical voting between one election and the next. That is far less important than the total amount of tactical voting already in the system, in the widest sense of voting that is or has been influenced by the voters' or the parties' perceptions of the candidates' chances of winning. This could only be measured by a long-term study of voters' behaviour over several elections, but one can get an idea of the extent of it by comparing the behaviour of voters in different seats.

Putney and Richmond are neighbouring seats in south-west London with broadly similar social profiles, although Richmond is a little more solidly middle-class and Putney has a few more council tenants. The Conservative vote has traditionally been the same in both seats, but the non-Conservative vote is completely different. The Conservatives won them both in 1992 but Putney is now Labour and Richmond Park is a Liberal Democrat seat. Even members of the Labour Party have been known to vote Liberal Democrat in Richmond and Liberal Democrat members have been known to vote Labour in Putney. Yet if you go from one to the other, there is little discernible difference in the character of the area.

In seats like Richmond Park or Newbury it is difficult to see how Labour can ever regain second place. Once it has dropped into third place, third-party squeeze acts as a ratchet to keep the Labour vote down. The better the Liberal Democrats' chances of winning the seat, the harder the Labour vote is squeezed. If it is squeezed right down to its core and the Liberal Democrats still do not win the seat, ex-Labour supporters may come to the conclusion that there is no longer any point in voting Liberal and go back to Labour, as they did in a number of southern seats in the last election. But this is only likely to happen in seats where neither the Liberal Democrats nor Labour stands a realistic chance of defeating the Tories.

Thus there are a great many seats across the South where Labour is locked into third place and can do little more than play a spoiling game. This is particularly true of agricultural rural areas and affluent commuter areas in the South. It is less true of the more industrial southern towns, such as Gloucester and Stroud, where Labour won in 1997, or the larger southern cities such as Plymouth, Exeter, Southampton and Brighton, where Labour's strong position after the 1992 general election led to victories in 1997. But it is becoming more true in affluent towns such as Cheltenham, Bath, Windsor and Eastbourne. There are, in effect, blue-yellow areas and blue-red areas in the south: affluent and agricultural areas are blue-yellow while industrial and new towns are blue-red.

As a result there is now a large chameleon electorate in the south that will vote Labour in one area, Liberal Democrat in another. They are the same sort of people with the same concerns and the same political views, but they vote differently in different areas. They may also vote differently in different elections. Very often they will vote Labour in district or county elections because there is a pocket of Labour voters in their area big enough to elect a Labour councillor, but Liberal Democrat in the Westminster or European elections because Labour cannot realistically hope to win the seat. There was evidence in 1997, when the local elections were held on the same day as the general election, that split-ticket voting occurred. In Bristol West, for example, the Liberal Democrats failed to win the parliamentary seat and saw their percentage vote decline, yet they did well in the local elections on the same day, taking one seat from Labour and one from the Conservatives.

If we look back at the 1993 county council elections and the Newbury by-election, these represented a triumph for the voter over the voting system. The voters succeeded in removing the Tories from county halls they had controlled for over a century in the south and leaving them in control of only one of the 39 English shires. They achieved this by the tactic of voting Labour where Labour could win and Liberal Democrat where Liberal Democrat could win. That tended to be Labour north of the M4 and Liberal Democrat south of the M4, but for the voters it was just a question of which was the most effective way to beat the Tories. This trend continued in the European elections of 1994 and the local elections from there on. In Scotland the local elections of 1995 fought on new boundaries for the new unitary authorities which were thought of as being helpful to the Conservatives produced no Conservative councils at all.

The part played by the political parties in this was minimal. Although in Berkshire in 1993 there was some discussion between Labour and the Liberal Democrats over a possible pact, the talks broke down. Labour candidates withdrew in two seats, but that was a result of unilateral action. In Oxfordshire there was also some discussion between the parties over which seats to fight. But the decisive part was played by the voters. As the BBC reporter James Cox put it: "The increasingly sophisticated electorate invented their own de facto pacts, choosing the candidate most likely to ditch the Tories."

This has created a new paradigm for politics in large parts of the country in which the electorate treat Labour and the Liberal Democrats as alternatives. Instead of a three-party system there are two main two-party systems, a Con-Lab and a Con-Lib system. Supporters of FPTP often claim that their system gives voters a clear choice between the effective contenders for government. If this were true, it would be an argument in the system's favour. But sadly it is not. In 227 of the 659 seats the voters do not have a straight choice between Conservative and Labour. They are asked to choose between Conservative and Liberal Democrat or between Labour and SNP, but they are not asked to make the choice that really matters, between Conservative and Labour. The electoral system has become like a court case where the witness is asked any question but the right question.

Before the 1997 election, the right question would have been: "Do you want a Conservative government?" and the overwhelming answer would be "No". A poll by ICM in the *Guardian* in March 1993 showed that 65 per cent of people would vote for joint candidates supported by Labour and the Liberal Democrats, more than the combined total of those who would vote Labour and Liberal Democrat. The trouble was that a majority could vote for Labour and the Liberal Democrats and the country would still be left with a Conservative government as it was in 1992. But that never materialised.

The shire county elections created a new political situation where many English counties have no overall control. This has three consequences. First, supporters of FPTP can no longer argue that their system delivers majority government. It clearly does not. The age of the hung council is here and a hung parliament can never be ruled out. John Major came very close to having one when he ran out of his overall majority on the night of the Wirral South by-election. Second, political parties will have to get used to consensus and cooperation as a far more important ingredient in their relations with other parties than it was in the past. The local councils in which no party is in overall control will be a laboratory for a new politics. Thirdly, people of all political persuasions will have to accept that the adversarial tradition in British politics may no longer be the best model for the future.

Many MPs like the adversarial ethos of the House of Commons and believe it springs from the FPTP system. In fact this ethos may have far more to do with majority government and with the fact that so many MPs are men. The breakthrough for women in 1997, when 120 women were elected to parliament, including a woman Speaker, Betty Boothroyd, was partly a result of Labour's strategy of all-women shortlists which were judged illegal and had to be abandoned. Many of those women are in marginal seats which risk being lost at the next election. Although there are double the number of women elected in 1992, there are still less than one in five women in the Commons. More than half the number of women ever elected as MPs, since women over 30 won the vote in 1918, are there today.

We could say that the disproportionality is caused not so much by the FPTP system as by the use of single-member constituencies. It is mistakenly believed that the single-member constituency is part of the British democratic tradition, but in fact it is less than 100 years old. The parliament of Simon de Montfort consisted of two-member seats and this remained the standard pattern for six centuries. From 1832 there were three- and even four- member seats. It is only since 1885 that the majority of MPs have represented single-member constituencies and only since 1950 that all have represented them.

Academic research has shown that when a political party is choosing a list of candidates it is more likely to select women and ethnic minority candidates to balance the ticket, but when selecting a single candidate it is more likely to choose a man. It is more likely to choose women and ethnic minority candidates in three-member council seats where all the seats are fought at the same time. It is also more likely to choose women and ethnic minority candidates in countries which have regional lists. In Germany far more women candidates are selected and far more women MPs are elected in the list section than in the constituency section of their additional member system (AMS). Labour will find it harder to elect more women MPs, or even retain those it has, if it continues to support a system based entirely on single-member constituencies. This includes the alternative vote (AV) and the supplementary vote (SV) systems. If Labour adopts an AMS system following the referendum, it will find it easier to emulate its sister party, the SPD, which has set itself a target of 40 per cent women's representation.

Even under the FPTP system it was sometimes easier for women to be selected when there were two-member seats, before 1950. In 1945 Barbara Castle was elected as the second Labour MP for the two-member seat of Blackburn and said that, as a woman, she would never have been selected if it had not been a two-member seat and the other candidate, already chosen, had not been a man.

Given the clear distortions in the representation of parties and people, it is hard to understand why the system has not been changed to make votes count. For that we need to look at and learn from our history.

THE ROAD TO
ELECTORAL REFORM

9 THE PAST: UP TO 1945

The basic idea that constituencies elect the candidates who have the highest number of votes has been accepted since Simon de Montfort summoned the Commons to Lewes in 1265. But the Lewes Parliament had very little power and the idea of an election was simply to choose people to represent the territorial interest of each borough and county, not to debate ways of running the country. It may have been a satisfactory system for choosing burgesses to represent boroughs. But the function of these burgesses was to defend the interests of their boroughs at a time when people saw their interests entirely in territorial terms. If the king wanted to raise a tax to pay for a war, he wanted to know whether the merchants of York, Winchester or Durham would support him. It was only much later that elections began to involve a choice of parties or governments.

Until 1832 there were so many irregularities and abuses that people hardly thought of it as a voting system. Only after the Great Reform Act had begun to establish a rough equality in constituency size did people begin to think about electoral issues, such as the way in which votes were translated into seats or who should be entitled to vote. The Act for the first time defined voters as men. Reform of the voting system and the extension of the franchise became popular issues for the first time and were linked with other popular, radical issues. The supporters of the Bill had campaigned for both "bread and votes".

In the 1840s and 1850s people started to point to the shortcomings of the electoral system and advocate change. Thomas Hare advocated a more proportional system in his pamphlet, *The Machinery of Representation*, in 1857. John Stuart Mill took up his cause in *Considerations on Representative Government* in 1861. Mill acted as Hare's propagandist and spread the idea rapidly. It was taken up in Australia by Catherine Spence who published a pamphlet in 1861, *A Plea for Pure Democracy*, applying the ideas of proportional representation (PR) to electoral districts instead of to a single national constituency, and laying the foundations of the single transferable vote (STV).

In the following decade there was a debate between Mill who argued for PR and Walter Bagehot who defended the existing system. Mill believed that proportional representation would "secure representation in proportion to numbers … and secondly, no elector would be … represented by someone whom he had not chosen". But Bagehot argued that the purpose of elections was to elect not just representatives but governments, so it did not matter if people were represented by MPs they had not chosen. He also feared that PR would lead to "the return of party men…bound hard and fast with party bands and fetters". He took comfort in the thought that, although he could never hope that his vote would elect a Liberal MP in a Tory area, there were probably equal numbers of Tory voters wasting their votes in Liberal areas.

Politicians were by no means committed to the FPTP system. The former Whig prime minister Lord John Russell supported Lord Cairns's amendment to the 1867 Reform Bill for an early form of PR, 'limited vote', to be applied in the larger counties and cities that had three- and four-member seats. The counties that qualified for three members were Berkshire, Buckinghamshire, Cambridgeshire, Dorset, Herefordshire, Hertfordshire and Oxfordshire. The cities were Birmingham, Leeds, Liverpool, Manchester and Glasgow. The City of London qualified for four.

Disraeli supported the limited vote in the Commons. The idea was that voters were to have only two votes in three-member seats and three votes in four-member seats. The effect of this is to give the minority party a chance of picking up one seat in each constituency. When people have three votes in a three-member seat, as they do still in local elections in some parts of England, then the same party usually wins all three seats. But if the voters have only two votes, then the leading party can only be sure of winning two seats and the second party has a good chance of picking up the third seat.

This can be seen in the following examples. If voters have three votes for three seats, the same party wins all three seats as in example (a). If voters have two votes to split between three candidates, then both parties may collect only two-thirds of their previous vote (b). But if the smaller party is clever, it will put up only two candidates, forcing its voters to concentrate their forces on only two candidates and winning two seats (c). The first party's only course is to put up two candidates itself, taking two seats but leaving the third seat to the other party (d).

TABLE 9.1   **LIMITED VOTE**

	(a)	*(b)*	*(c)*	*(d)*
Elected	Con 51	Con 34	Lab 49	Con 51
	Con 51	Con 34	Lab 49	Con 51
	Con 51	Con 34	Con 34	Lab 49
Not elected	Lab 49	Lab 32	Con 34	Lab 49
	Lab 49	Lab 32	Con 34	
	Lab 49	Lab 32		

As a voting system it had advantages over FPTP. It was less likely to give one party all the seats in an area. It represented not only majorities but some minorities in parliament. When it was debated in the Commons, it was opposed by diehard defenders of the FPTP system using almost exactly the same arguments that they use today. The Earl of Malmesbury told the Lords: "The mind of an Englishman is a very straightforward piece of machinery. He is accustomed ever to obey majorities and to be obedient to the decisions and verdicts of majorities." But for the first and so far the only time in history parliament successfully voted for a change in the voting system for general elections. The limited vote was introduced. However, it was not long before its drawbacks became apparent. Parties could only maximise their seats if they persuaded the voters to spread their support evenly between the parties' candidates. This gave an advantage to the party that was better able to organise its supporters. The Birmingham Liberal caucus

learned how to do this most effectively and ensured that almost no
Conservatives were elected in Birmingham between 1867 and 1885.

This fault could have been rectified by making votes transferable between candidates of the same party. Indeed it is an interesting historical 'if' that Gladstone seriously considered introducing STV. In the end
he decided, wrongly as it turned out, that the best way of ensuring that
minorities were represented was to turn the three- and four-member
constituencies into single-member constituencies. Both parties turned
against the limited vote and it was abolished in the Redistribution of
Seats Act of 1885 by removing the three- and four-member seats.

It was then that the voting system took the shape that it has today
as a plurality or FPTP system based on single-member constituencies.
Some two-member seats persisted through to 1950 along with 12 university seats that were elected by STV. Even now FPTP is not universal
in the UK, as STV is used for European and local elections in Northern
Ireland. Elections in the future will use proportional systems for the
Scottish Parliament, Welsh and London Assemblies and for the European Parliament.

But in the 19th century FPTP was less distorting than it is now. In
the great majority of constituencies there were only two parties, the
Liberals and the Conservatives. Between the two great extensions of
the franchise in 1832 and 1884 there was no election where fewer than
98.6 per cent of the candidates in England, Scotland and Wales were
either Conservative or Liberal, many of them uncontested. In the great
battle between Gladstone and Disraeli in 1874, there were nearly
1,000 Conservative and Liberal candidates and only one standing for
any other party. He got two votes.

It was only after 1884, when many working men were enfran-
chised, that there were more third-party candidates, some of them
standing as Labour, but, apart from a few Independent Liberals in
1885, they never reached 1 per cent of the vote in England, Scotland
and Wales until the 1900 election. Thus there was not only less debate
about voting systems in the 19th century, there was less to complain
about. Supporters of defeated candidates may have felt aggrieved that

they were unrepresented in parliament, but they had no worries about wasted votes, tactical voting or third-party squeeze.

TABLE 9.2   **CANDIDATES IN SOME PRE-1900 ELECTIONS**

	Con	Lib	Other	Irish
1835	407	538	0	0
1847	422	393	9	55
1857	351	507	1	19
1865	406	516	0	0
1874	507	489	1	83
1886	563	449	4	99
1895	588	447	40	105

Only in Ireland did voters encounter the quirks that appear when a system best suited to two parties is contested by three. There the Conservatives and Liberals were challenged and eventually eclipsed by the Home Rulers who were considerably helped by the voting system. In 1874 they won fewer votes than the Tories but nearly twice as many seats. In 1880 they again won fewer votes but nearly three times as many seats. In 1886 they were again behind in votes but took five times as many seats, most of them unopposed. The Liberals saw their vote squeezed to almost nothing.

TABLE 9.3   **VOTES AND SEATS IN IRELAND, 1874–86**

	Votes (%)			Seats (total 101)			
	Con	Lib	Nat	Con	Lib	Nat	Unopposed
1874	41	18	40	31	10	60	18
1880	40	23	38	23	15	63	15
1886	50	1	49	17	0	84	69

The rise of democratic consciousness which led to the formation of the Social Democratic Federation in 1883 and the Fabian Society in 1884 also led to the foundation of the Proportional Representation Society in the same year. It started with 105 members and an income of £1,300. There was a considerable overlap in the appeal of these causes, because it was the movement for working-class representation that first demonstrated the shortcomings of the system. In the elections of the 1840s and 1850s the only other candidates in England, Scotland and Wales had been the Chartists. They won their only seat in 1847 and it is fair to say that they were not beaten by the land-owners or the factory-owners. They were beaten by the voting system. It crushed the spirit out of them.

Later in the 1860s the Reform League promoted working men under the banner of Liberalism. But the same thing happened in 1868. The Tories won one MP for every 5,000 votes. The Reform League won no seats at all in spite of winning 15,000 votes. Their votes were spread among seven candidates and none were elected.

In 1874 there were 13 Liberals standing in the labour interest, but only two were elected. In 1895 the Independent Labour Party (ILP) put up 28 candidates but they won no seats even though they won 44,325 votes, which would have been enough to elect four Liberal MPs in that election. In 1900 the infant Labour Representation Committee took 62,698 votes, enough to elect eight Tories or ten Liberals, but only two Labour MPs were elected.

Keir Hardie, the party's first leader, was in favour of PR, largely because he wanted Labour to have its own identity distinct from the Liberals. He saw a change in the voting system as a way of preventing the party from being subsumed by the Liberals. Indeed, leading figures of both the main socialist organisations that came together to form the Labour Representation Committee in 1900 were advocates of PR, including Philip Snowden, William Crawford Anderson and George Roberts of the Independent Labour Party and Harry Quelch of the Social Democratic Federation. So were Mary Macarthur, one of the most prominent early women trade unionists, Millicent Fawcett, the suffragist, Eleanor Rathbone, the social reformer, and Kate Courtney, sister of Beatrice Webb.

The 1900 election and subsequent by-elections made it clear that Liberal and Labour candidates spoiled one another's chances. In March 1903 Herbert Gladstone, the Liberal whip, and Ramsay MacDonald, the Labour leader, agreed a secret memorandum under which the Liberals would stand down in Labour's favour in certain seats and Labour would not stand in Liberal-held seats.

Both party leaders had trouble in forcing recalcitrant local parties not to put up candidates in by-elections without telling them of the existence of the pact, but it paid off handsomely in the 1906 election. Labour put up only 50 candidates, and won 29 seats, 24 of them without opposition from the Liberals. According to Henry Pelling, historian of the Labour Party, the secret deal with the Liberals was by far the most important explanation of their success. The best evidence for that was in Scotland, where the Scottish Liberal Federation refused any compromise with Labour and as a consequence the Liberals forfeited six seats they might otherwise have won in Scotland and Labour won only two out of ten seats it contested north of the border. The contrast was clear with England and Wales where the Liberals had won a landslide.

This secret pact with the Liberals helped the Labour Party to grow rapidly in the years from 1906 to 1910 and to play its part in supporting the introduction of the first pensions and benefits that laid the foundations of the welfare state. The pact remained in force in the two elections of 1910 when the Labour Party restricted its candidates to 78 and 56 by arrangement with Asquith's Liberals. Without this arrangement the Conservatives might have won and the battle to restrict the powers of the House of Lords and establish the supremacy of the Commons might have been lost.

Neither the Liberal nor the Labour Party ever acknowledged the role that this pact played in their fortunes, but it did help to raise interest in PR in the Labour Party. When the pact started to break down, it forced the party to consider the issue of voting systems. The 1913

Labour conference saw a debate between supporters of PR and supporters of the alternative vote (AV). The executive felt it was "not in a position to decide between the two principles put forward" and called a special conference in 1914 to resolve the issue. The argument used by supporters of PR was the one that had convinced Hardie: that they did not want to be dependent on a Lib-Lab pact. F. Knee of the London Trades Council asked the conference: "Was any of the Labour members satisfied with the terms under which he sat in the House of Commons? In a large number of cases if a Liberal candidate was put up at the next election, the Labour man would be ousted. A Labour man ought to be dependent on Labour votes only and that could only be done under proportional representation." But the new party leader, Ramsay MacDonald, argued passionately against PR. His reasoning might seem rather curious today. "Opinions should not be coddled in their infancy; they should have to surmount reasonable obstacles. Every opinion which claimed parliamentary recognition should be asked to prove its staying power." As well as being leader, MacDonald was regarded as the party's leading intellectual and his views carried weight. The motion was lost by 1,400,000 to 700,000.

Despite MacDonald, support was growing. Resolutions in favour of electoral reform were passed at the Trades Union Congress in 1911 and 1913, at the Scottish TUC in 1912 and at the ILP conference in 1913. At the TUC Will Thorne, leader of the General and Municipal Workers, said it was difficult to understand why a proposal so pronouncedly democratic should ever have been regarded with any coldness by members of the labour and socialist movements. It seemed that rank-and-file members had much less difficulty understanding proportional electoral systems than many MPs. But the intellectual wing of the movement was opposed to reform. The Fabians were particularly hostile. A 1911 tract by Henry H. Schloesser, later an MP under the name Henry Slesser, emphasised the need for strong government and a voting system that would "accentuate the majority".

There was a majority in favour of reform among Labour MPs, among Liberal MPs, indeed in both the Commons and the Lords. But as so often happens in parliament, measures which are supported by a majority fail to pass into law because of the arcane workings of parliamentary procedure. A Speaker's Conference set up in 1916 recommended a mixture of STV and AV. In 1917 there was a free vote in the Commons on this hybrid system. STV was lost by 149 votes to 141, a majority of eight. Later AV was carried by 125 to 124, a majority of one. In January 1918 the Lords threw out AV and reinstated STV by 131 votes to 42, a majority of 89. In February the Commons reinstated AV by 195 to 194, again a majority of one, with all Liberal and Labour MPs voting in favour of AV. The conflict between an STV Lords and an AV Commons was not finally resolved until, with minutes to go before the bill ran out of time, both sides agreed to back down in favour of the status quo.

In 1918 the Labour Party conference voted in favour of PR and the TUC followed suit by voting for electoral reform in 1921 and 1922. Both motions, moved by the National Union of Clerks, called not only for the proportional representation of all opinions and interests by means of STV with constituencies returning at least five members, but also for the closing of public houses during the hours of polling.

Criticism of the voting system was strengthened by the bizarre results of the 1922, 1923 and 1924 elections (see Table 9.4 on the following page). In 1922 the Conservatives were elected with a huge majority over all other parties on just 38.5 per cent of the vote, the lowest winning share of the vote in parliament's history. In 1923 the Conservative vote fell by just 0.5 of a percentage point but they lost 86 seats. Conversely, Labour's vote went up by 1 percentage point but its seats increased by a third. Ramsay MacDonald found himself in Downing Street as prime minister in the first minority Labour government. After a year of Labour government, Labour's vote actually went up from 30.7 to 33.3 per cent in the 1924 election but its seats decreased from 191 to 151 and it lost power. It was a demonstration of the fact that FPTP can work in erratic and irrational ways.

TABLE 9.4   ELECTION RESULTS, 1922, 1923 AND 1924

615 seats	Majority = 308				
	1922	*1923*	+/-	*1924*	+/-
Con vote %	38.5	38.0	– 0.5	46.8	+ 8.8
Con seats	344	258	– 86	412	+ 154
Con seats %	55.9	42.0	– 14.0	67.0	+ 25.0
Lab vote %	29.7	30.7	+ 1.0	33.3	+ 2.6
Lab seats	142	191	+ 49	151	– 40
Lab seats %	23.1	31.1	+ 8.0	24.6	– 6.5
Lib vote %	28.8	29.7	+ 0.9	17.8	– 11.9
Lib seats	115	158	+ 43	40	– 118
Lib seats %	18.7	25.7	+ 7.0	6.5	– 19.2

The first Labour minority government, formed in 1924, did not pursue the issue of electoral reform, partly because in the 1923 general election it had been the beneficiary of the biggest jackpot the system had ever produced – a net switch of 67 seats on a swing of just 0.75 per cent – but also because Labour MPs were becoming confident that they could not only overtake the Liberals but replace them. Already in 1923 the voting system was far kinder to Labour than the Liberals. In votes Labour was only 1 percentage point ahead of the Liberals (30.7:29.7) but 33 seats ahead (191:158).

This would have been the historic opportunity to change the voting system if the Liberals had become convinced that they were on the losing side of this bargain before the Labour Party began to believe it was on the winning side. But, as G.R. Searle wrote in his history of the Liberal Party: "The fact is that the Liberals only became keen about electoral reform during the course of 1924 when they started to worry in earnest about their long-term survival. But this very situation meant that Labour's former support for electoral reform quickly evaporated. Why should Labour have made its own quest for power more difficult by throwing out a lifeline in the direction of the Liberals?"

Lloyd George had only himself to blame as it was largely his fault that PR had not been passed in 1918. His election manifesto had promised to carry out the recommendations of the Speaker's conference and the Speaker's conference had come out for a proportional system. But Lloyd George changed his mind and insisted on a free vote which led to the constitutional deadlock in which the clause was finally dropped. In 1925 he said to C.P. Scott, editor of the *Manchester Guardian*, that he felt he had made a great mistake in 1918. As Jenifer Hart wrote in her history of PR, he told Scott: "Someone ought to have come to him and gone into the whole matter, as he could have carried it then." But it was too late. The tide had turned.

A Fabian pamphlet by Herman Finer, which appeared in May 1924, argued that, although the results of the last two elections had been perverse because of the number of three-cornered contests: "Our electoral system suffers from temporary dislocation rather than permanent error. As it is likely that within 15 years the Liberal Party will be defunct, we shall then be troubled with fewer of such multiple-candidate contests."

In May 1924 a private member's bill in favour of PR was defeated. The opposition was led by a young MP and protégé of MacDonald, Herbert Morrison, on the grounds that he wanted government to be strong. He told the Commons he would prefer a bad government if strong and logical to one that wobbled. The bill was defeated by 238 to 144. Nearly all the Liberals voted for; the Conservatives against; and Labour voted 28 for and 89 against. A majority of MacDonald's cabinet voted in favour, but the bill's defeat persuaded them that there was no point in taking the issue any further.

Indeed, at the 1926 Labour conference the party's support for PR was overturned, although the party remained on the whole in favour of AV. The 1929 elections produced a Labour minority government with fewer votes than the Conservatives but more seats. The government had no manifesto commitment to electoral reform but introduced the subject into the King's speech: "My Government propose to institute an examination of the election so that the workings of the law relating to parliamentary elections may be brought into conformity with the new conditions." A Speaker's conference was set up under Lord Ullswater, who as Speaker Lowther had chaired the 1916–17 Speaker's conference. When that failed to agree, Labour nevertheless went ahead with a Representation of the People Bill which, among other things, would introduce AV. There is no doubt that this was widely supported in the party.

At the meeting of the National Executive in December 1930 Arthur Henderson, the Foreign Secretary, asked the executive to give its "approval or acquiescence" to the bill and the motion was passed by 16 votes to three. It was subsequently endorsed in the parliamentary Labour Party by 133 votes to 20. The bill passed through all its stages in the Commons by 278 to 228 on a whipped vote with all Labour and Liberal MPs in favour. But the House of Lords sent the bill back with a wrecking amendment that excluded boroughs from the provision of the bill if they had populations of less than 200,000 – which included most of the boroughs with Tory MPs. That delayed the bill for long enough to ensure that it collapsed when MacDonald formed a national government and called an election in the autumn of 1931.

Thus another historic opportunity to change the voting system was lost. In both 1918 and 1930 it came tantalisingly close. On both occasions the Commons, left to itself, would have adopted AV. This time MacDonald could have pushed the bill through in the dying days of the parliament, but chose not to. Nearly 70 years were to pass before the opportunity would present itself again. Indeed for the best part of a century change has been frustrated because only one of the three main parties has supported it. Until the 1920s it was the Labour Party. Since then it has been the Liberals. Unfortunately the Liberals converted to it just as Labour was losing interest. It was clear that change would only come when two of the three main parties came to the conclusion that the FPTP system could no longer be defended and either one or both of those parties had a majority in the Commons.

Perhaps it was poetic justice that the Labour Party, having missed its chance of changing the system, suffered very badly from it in the 1931 election. Its share of the vote dropped less than one-sixth from 37 to 31 per cent, but its seats collapsed by nearly five-sixths from 287 to 52. In 1935 Labour's vote recovered to 38 per cent – higher than in 1992 – but it still won only 154 seats. One could say that Labour's traumas in the 1930s owed more to the vagaries of the voting system than to MacDonald's treachery. But that is not how it was seen at the time. The prevailing mood seems to have been that the voting system was a gamble and Labour should wait for its luck to turn. After the 1935 election Arthur Greenwood pointed to the 429 government MPs and cheerfully told the 154 Labour MPs: "A very small turnover of votes ... might, through the accidents of our electoral system, have put us there and them here."

His arithmetic was faulty. It would have taken a large swing in votes to reverse the result. But his gambler's instinct was unmistakable. As the party secretary, J.S. Middleton, said after the election: "There is no greater gamble on earth than a British general election."

Philip Snowden, who became one of MacDonald's National Labour supporters, blamed his old party for its own predicament. It should have introduced PR when it had the chance. He wrote in 1934: "They appear to be expecting that the general election will give them the advantage of the gamble and the chance of winning seats to which they are not entitled on the actual votes they have polled."

Essentially that is the issue we are still discussing today: whether the gamble Labour took on the electoral system in the 1930s was right then or is right now.

The debate continued up until the end of the war. Under the wartime truce the three coalition parties agreed not to put up candidates against one another in by-elections, but the Labour, Liberal and church leaders jointly supported Jennie Lee as candidate in Bristol Central in 1943 against the Conservative candidate. She stood on a platform of total support for the recently published report, "Social Insurance and Allied Services", by the Liberal, Sir William Beveridge. "I stand for every word, letter and comma in the Beveridge Report," she said.

At the 1943 Labour Party conference the Leyton Trades Council delegate H.R. (Reg) Underhill called for an inquiry into electoral systems in terms that could still apply today. He told delegates:

"Many of you from rural or semi-rural areas know that there are millions of voters today who are not adequately represented. In the Southern Counties there are about 79 seats of which Labour holds nil, and yet we have a vast number of votes in those areas. We want significance given to every single vote cast by the electorate."

Reg Underhill went on to become the National Agent of the Labour Party and a staunch defender of FPTP. After he retired he became a member of the Plant Commission and chaired its subcommittee on voter participation. Like some other members of the Plant Commission he was convinced by the evidence and became a supporter of a mixed-member system. He told the Lords on January 20th 1993 that the time had come "seriously to consider whether we should change from FPTP". Sadly he died in March 1993, two weeks before the Plant Commission took its decision.

10 THE 'GOLDEN ERA': 1945–1970s

The decisive result of the 1945 election put the issue of electoral reform to the very bottom of the political agenda where it stayed for the next 30 years. One could accuse the Labour Party of a lack of principle in losing interest in reform of the voting system as soon as it discovered it could win an outright majority in the Commons and enjoy the power of untrammelled one-party government. But it would be fair to add that the FPTP system exhibited fewer faults in the late 1940s and 1950s than at any time since 1900.

Labour's support was distributed more evenly around the country after the 1945 election than at any election before or since. H.R. Underhill's fear that Labour would never win representation in the southern counties or rural areas appeared misplaced as the 1945 results came in. The 1997 election saw Labour win back many rural or mixed-rural seats that it had not held since the great post-war election, such as Harwich, Kettering, St Albans, Shipley, Sittingbourne and Stroud. But most of New Labour's rural seats are built round an industrial core and it has not reached into the agricultural heartlands of England in the way that the Labour Party did in 1945. Among the seats that returned Labour MPs at the end of the war were Cambridgeshire, Harborough, Sudbury, Taunton and Winchester, all of them seats where Labour still struggles to get out of third place. As Herbert Morrison said after the 1945 victory, it was the election in which Labour became a truly national party.

For the next two decades Britain seemed to revert to the two-party system of Gilbert and Sullivan when "every boy and every gal, that's born into the world alive, is either a little Liberal, or else a little Conservative", except that Labour had now replaced the Liberals. Over 96 per cent of voters supported one of the two main parties in both 1951 and 1955. It seemed as though the three-party contests and hung par-

liaments produced by the inter-war elections had just been a trans-
itional phenomenon while Labour and the Liberals fought to become
the main challenger to the Conservatives. From now on the system
would be stable.

Certainly the phenomena of tactical voting and third-party squeeze
were almost unknown to the two main parties in the 1940s and 1950s.
If people were Tories, they voted Tory and if they were Labour, they
voted Labour, and that was that. To be sure, if they were Liberals they
might not have had a Liberal candidate and would have had to vote for
a second-choice party. But for the rest of the electorate the system
seemed to work.

It was the 1951 election that may have rekindled the disillusion because it demonstrated the perversity of the voting system. Labour won
what still remains today its highest vote in a general election,
13,948,833, and the second highest vote that any party has won in an
election. More importantly it was 230,684 votes more than the
13,718,199 that the Conservatives won in the same election. Yet it was
Churchill not Attlee who formed the government, because the Conservatives had won 321 seats to Labour's 295.

Not many people paid attention to the parties' overall shares of the
vote in those days and indeed the figures need to be adjusted to take account of the fact that four Conservatives were returned unopposed as
Conservative Unionists in Northern Ireland. But it illustrated that FPTP
could still go wrong even in the most favourable conditions with two-
party contests in the great majority of seats. The reasons for this perverse result were that Labour's vote was very inefficiently distributed
with many huge majorities piled up in safe seats, and the boundary
commission had built a slight Tory bias into the system by drawing
smaller constituencies in rural than in urban areas.

Much is made of the fact that the Liberal vote dwindled to 2.6 per
cent in 1951 and 2.7 per cent in 1955. These were by far the lowest
percentages that any of the main parties suffered in any election this
century, unless one counts Labour's vote in 1900, the year it was
founded. But it would be a mistake to think that Liberal support had

disappeared or that it had been relegated to a few Celtic outposts in the
early 1950s. That is an illusion. What happened was that the Liberals
temporarily stopped putting up candidates in the majority of constituencies. Even in 1945 they stood in fewer than half the seats, leaving those people determined not to vote Conservative with no option
but to vote Labour. In 1951 they stood in 109 of the 630 seats. In
1955 they stood in 110, barely one-fifth of the total, mainly because
the local Liberal Associations could not raise the £150 deposit. This
artificially depressed the Liberal vote to the lowest levels it ever
reached, 2.6 per cent in 1951 and 2.7 per cent in 1955, and boosted
the two main parties' share of the vote to 96.8 and 96.1 per cent.
Labour politicians believed that the Liberals were on their way to
oblivion and Labour would take their place in a new golden era of the
two-party system that would place them in power as often and for as
long as the Whigs in the 19th century. But reports of the strange death
of Liberal England, to quote the title of George Dangerfield's book,
were exaggerated. The voting system had only temporarily depressed
the Liberal vote.

In a series of calculations Michael Steed has shown that, even
though the Liberals' share of the vote dropped to 2.6 per cent in 1951,
their support was four times higher. If they had been able to stand in
every seat their share of the popular vote would have been 11 per cent
rather than 2.6 per cent in 1951 and 7.5 per cent rather than 2.7 per
cent in 1955. Indeed, the Liberal vote per candidate was 14.7 per cent
in 1951. It was just the number of Liberal candidates that was low.
Liberal fortunes picked up again in 1953–54 and rose steadily from
then on. As soon as Liberals found the money to stand in most constituencies, 517 in February 1974 and 619 in October 1974, their vote
was again up in the upper teens and lower twenties where it has been
ever since. The heyday of the two-party system, the 'golden era' to
which Labour nostalgists look back, may have been little more than a
statistical mirage.

In 1954 a new phenomenon appeared which was equally a product
of the voting system. In the Inverness by-election the Conservatives

held the seat but Labour was pushed from second to third place. The Liberals, who had not even put up a candidate in the previous election, captured second place. That was the first time that the Liberals demonstrated their ability to squeeze other parties in a by-election. It was the Liberals who had traditionally been made to suffer third-party squeeze at the hands of Conservatives and Labour but now they were showing that they could turn the tables and put the squeeze on Labour. In 1958 the Liberals went one better in Torrington in Devon, not only pushing Labour into third place but pushing the Tories into second place and taking the seat. In 1962 they won Orpington in Kent. The Liberal by-election surge had arrived and the Liberal revival was under way.

In February 1974 the Conservatives suffered the same galling experience as Labour had in 1951, when they won more votes than Labour in the election but saw Labour emerge with more seats and Harold Wilson taking power. In October 1974 they had the further depressing experience of seeing their vote sink to 35.8 per cent, their lowest since 1859. These two experiences – of feeling robbed in February 1974 and humiliated in October 1974 – left the Conservatives feeling completely disillusioned with the voting system. It led to the establishment in 1975 of a Tory pressure group, Conservative Action for Electoral Reform (CAER), which claimed the support at one stage of some 70 Tory MPs, including Douglas Hurd and Chris Patten. In 1976 Lord Hailsham spoke of 'elective dictatorship' in his Dimbleby lecture. A parallel campaign was set up called the Labour Study Group for Electoral Reform, which Austin Mitchell joined after his by-election victory in 1977. It campaigned for a proportional system to be used for the election of the European Parliament. After the 1979 election defeat this group was renamed the Labour Campaign for Electoral Reform (LCER). The campaign to change the voting system was under way.

11 THE PLANT PROCESS: 1987–93

Despite the formation of the Labour Campaign for Electoral Reform (LCER), Labour's revival of interest in the subject did not begin in earnest until their third consecutive defeat in 1987. Labour conferences had never shown anything more than an insignificant level of support for electoral reform since the 1920s. But at the conference in 1987 there were 25 resolutions or amendments calling on the Labour Party to commit itself to reforming the electoral system.

Although this was brusquely dismissed from the platform by the party's deputy leader Roy Hattersley, two of his front-bench colleagues, Robin Cook and Jeff Rooker, spoke from the floor at a fringe meeting of the LCER and subsequently joined it. They were signed up by Ron Medlow, who had taken over as secretary of LCER after the 1983 general election when it had no more than a few dozen members and had helped to build up membership through a tireless round of meetings, recruitment, newsletters and model resolutions.

Electoral reform was ruled out of consideration in Labour's policy review, but it was being canvassed elsewhere. In July 1988 the Campaign for a Scottish Assembly launched its "Claim of Right for Scotland" which started a debate about a new voting system for a Scottish Parliament. In the following months there was a spate of articles and pamphlets about electoral reform. Patrick Dunleavy wrote an article, "Why Labour should think again", for the *New Statesman and Society*. Its editor, Stuart Weir, and Anthony Barnett started Charter 88 later that year. The Fabian Society published a pamphlet by Martin Linton called *Labour Can Still Win*, urging the party to reconsider its support of the electoral status quo. In January 1989, the *New Statesman and Society* published an article by Mary Georghiou, "Electoral Reform and Me", about a 1987 candidate's experience of fighting tactical voting in Bristol West and coming out in favour of electoral reform.

But little of this new thinking seemed to have reached the party leadership. In spring 1989 the party's policy document *Meet the Challenge, Make the Change* described the FPTP system as "the most honest, the most efficient and the most effective form of government". At the May National Executive meeting Robin Cook tried to have the whole section deleted, but received only four votes in support. But there were other straws in the wind. The Scottish Constitutional Convention held its first meeting in March. The Green Party won 2 million votes, 15 per cent of the vote, but no seats in the European elections in June. There were 43 resolutions and amendments on electoral reform at Labour's annual conference in October. The issue was at last beginning to move off the bottom of Labour's political agenda.

TABLE 11.1 **LABOUR CONFERENCE RESOLUTIONS AND AMENDMENTS ON ELECTORAL REFORM, 1987–91**

1987 Brighton	25 resolutions and amendments
1988 Blackpool	7 resolutions
1989 Brighton	37 resolutions and 6 amendments
1990 Blackpool	31 resolutions and 6 amendments
1991 Brighton	35 resolutions (30 for and 5 against)

At the 1989 conference the resolution on electoral reform was defeated by a substantial majority of three to one, but the losing side drew more comfort from the result than the winners. After all, 1,443,000 votes had been cast in the cause of electoral reform. Since it was known that only seven of the larger trade unions had voted for the motion, it was possible to calculate that about half of the constituency Labour parties must have voted for it. This was the first indication of the extent of support for electoral reform among Labour Party members.

From then on the LCER grew rapidly to become the largest campaigning group within the Labour Party, with 2,000 members and over 120 MPs on its list of sponsors. And although some of its opponents claimed that the campaign was born of despair, the fastest growth in LCER's membership came in fact between 1990 and 1991 when Labour was riding high in the polls and recording dramatic by-election victories against the Conservative government.

TABLE 11.2 **LCER MEMBERSHIP, 1984–93**

Date	No.
1984	35
1985	50
1986	100
1987	200
1988	300
1989	700
1990	1,000
1991	1,500
1992	1,700
1993	2,000

It was in 1990 that Labour moved from outright opposition to an agnostic position on electoral reform. The Fabians held a New Year School on Constitutional and Electoral Reform with Roy Hattersley in debate with Anthony Barnett. The Labour Coordinating Committee published a pamphlet called "Getting It In Proportion", advocating AMS. Richard Kuper of the Socialist Society published a booklet called *Electing for Democracy*. Helena Catt wrote "The Intelligent Person's Guide to Electoral Reform" in *New Statesman and Society*. In an article in the electoral reform edition of *Samizdat* Mary Georghiou argued that democracy should be Labour's elusive "big idea" and if the party were to adopt electoral reform it would be seen as a symbolic indication that the voters could trust Labour with power. "Labour needs to show it trusts the electorate if it expects the electorate to trust us. To get the trust it needs Labour will have to admit that some people do not just want a different government but to change the way the government is elected."

The first move came from an unexpected quarter. The Labour Party in Scotland had been the biggest beneficiary of the FPTP system, winning 69 per cent of the seats in Scotland in 1987 on 42 per cent of the vote, an even greater disproportionality than the national result which gave Margaret Thatcher 58 per cent of the seats for 42 per cent of the vote. Yet it was the Scottish Labour Party that decided at its Dunoon conference in March 1990 that it could not accept FPTP elections for the Scottish Parliament.

Neil Kinnock told the conference from the rostrum that this was the decision of a confident, not a defeatist, party. "Given our strong lead in political support in Scotland, no one can claim that our party is examining the detail of methods of electing the Scottish Assembly from any position of weakness or supplication. We are doing it from a position of strength and in the interests of democracy."

The Labour Party insisted that the choice of a voting system for the Scottish Parliament was an entirely different issue from an electoral system for the Commons, and in May the National Executive (NEC) stated explicitly in its policy document, *Looking to the Future*: "Labour is opposed to changing the electoral system for the House of Commons". What was not known at the time was that the party leader, Neil Kinnock, unwilling to adopt the hard line being taken by his deputy Roy Hattersley, had argued at a pre-NEC meeting that these words should be deleted, but lost.

Perhaps the most significant event of the year, as things turned out, was the decision of the National Executive to set up a working party to consider the type of voting system to be used for elections to the Scottish Parliament, the regional assemblies, the second chamber and the European Parliament. The LCER prompted a motion to the October conference welcoming the working party but asking for its terms of reference to be broadened to include elections to the House of Commons. Thus the battle at the party conference centred not on the issue of electoral reform itself but on the terms of reference of the working party. Roy Hattersley told television interviewers that he would be happy to accept new voting systems for Scotland, for the regions, for

Europe, but not for the House of Commons. The distinction began to sound tenuous. Ron Todd, general secretary of the TGWU and not a known supporter of electoral reform, argued on common sense grounds that the working party should be allowed to look at all voting systems. That tilted the balance and the motion was narrowly carried, against the recommendation of the platform, by 2,766,000 to 2,557,000.

The 1990 vote was undoubtedly a moral victory for the reformers and there was evidence that they were in a majority among ordinary party members. A survey of party members by two university researchers, Patrick Seyd and Paul Whiteley, found that when members were asked whether the electoral system "should be replaced by a system of proportional representation", there were 58 per cent in favour and only 31 per cent against. But that did not mean that the battle had been won. It was followed by a backlash in 1991. A First Past The Post Campaign was set up by the Campaign for Labour Party Democracy and chaired by Bob Cryer, MP. A similar grouping, the Scottish Labour Campaign for Electoral Success, was chaired by George Foulkes, MP. They warned of dire consequences if any reformed voting system were adopted.

The party leaders were happy to leave the issue to the working party, chaired by Raymond Plant, then professor at Southampton University, subsequently Master of St Catherine's College, Oxford. When it started work on 4 December 1990, it included only two known supporters of electoral reform for the House of Commons, Jeff Rooker and John Evans, and several people known or assumed to be supporters of FPTP. It considered the issue in depth, consulted the party and delivered its first interim report, *Democracy, Representation and Elections*, running to over 100 pages, in July 1991. It made no recommendations, but set out the options as a basis for further consultation.

The Plant Report, as it became known, was acclaimed as the most thorough and principled appraisal of voting systems undertaken by any political party. At the same time, the Institute for Public Policy Research published *The Constitution of the United Kingdom* which recommended the additional member system (AMS) for election of MPs to the Commons "in order that the proportion of the seats held by that party in the House in respect of that nation or region corresponds as closely as possible to the proportion that the votes cast for that party in the nation or region bear to the total votes cast there".

At the 1991 conference there were 35 resolutions on electoral reform, 30 for and five against. LCER supported a motion that simply welcomed the Plant Report and called on the party "to seize every opportunity to publicise and discuss Labour's new openness to electoral reform". The National Executive recommended acceptance and LCER found itself on the side of the majority. The motion was carried by 3,533,000 to 948,000. In the space of two years the party had reversed its 1989 decision.

In a New Year radio interview in 1992 Neil Kinnock gave a hint that he was now more sympathetic to electoral reform. He did not want to pre-empt the decision of the Plant Commission and remained non-committal. However, the working party had to recommend a voting system for the new Scottish Parliament. It recommended against FPTP and in favour of an additional member system (AMS). This was accepted by the January National Executive which also asked the Commission to work out a proportional voting system for the proposed Greater London Authority.

There were signs of movement in Labour's general election manifesto *It's time to get Britain working again*, which promised: "We will continue to encourage a wide and well informed public debate on the electoral system. The working party on electoral systems which we established in opposition under the distinguished chairmanship of Professor Raymond Plant will continue its work with an extended membership and enhanced authority and report to the next Labour government." Just a week before the election Neil Kinnock gave a stronger hint that there might be a change in the voting system. He offered to widen the Plant Commission beyond the confines of the Labour Party and spoke of government by consensus.

John Major played on the fears that a new voting system would mean a hung parliament. This was disingenuous since all the polls were indicating at the time that the country was heading towards a hung parliament under the existing voting system. But the Tory press took up his warning, the first sign of any real spirit in a lacklustre Conservative campaign, and turned it into a battle cry. The UK was said to be in mortal danger of a hung parliament and a weak, vacillating government if it voted for a change in the electoral system.

In a speech shortly afterwards Kenneth Baker warned that a change in the voting system might open the door to racist or fascist parties, citing the results of Land elections in Baden-Württemberg in Germany where the right-wing Republikaner party had won 11 per cent of the vote. "Under Neil, Nazi riots if Lab and Lib-Dem share power", was *The Sun*'s colourful headline on this story. Kenneth Baker also introduced race into the campaign by attacking the Labour and Liberal Democrat position on the Asylum Bill. The Tory newspapers seized on it. "Labour will open the floodgates to a wave of immigration," warned the *Daily Express*. "Baker's Migrant Flood Warning", screamed the front-page headline. The press failed to make much of the incongruity of a former home secretary who warned of a "wave of immigration" while attacking the threat of "racism" from PR. But in the final days of the campaign the Tory press was looking for any stick to beat Labour with.

PR was not a promising candidate in itself. In general the polls showed that people, if they had a view, were in favour. But hung parliaments were less popular and the Tory tabloids spent the last week of the campaign warning the voters of the evils of coalition governments which they claimed would be the inevitable result of any change in the voting system. By the end of the campaign PR had become the third most reported election issue in the tabloid press, quite an achievement for an issue that was hardly mentioned at all in the first three weeks of the campaign and is usually ignored by the tabloid papers.

If their objective was to turn the voters against hung parliaments, against PR and therefore against Neil Kinnock and the Liberal Democrats, they seemed to have succeeded. At the start of the campaign, according to the *Guardian*'s ICM poll in March, 41 per cent thought it would be a "good thing" if no party had an overall majority and 34 per cent thought it would be a "bad thing". The same question asked on polling day produced the opposite result: 31 per cent a "good thing" and 52 per cent a "bad thing".

An exit poll by NOP also asked voters whether they supported a change in the voting system and found more against than in favour. Asked whether they thought "we should scrap the present FPTP system for electing MPs and introduce PR", 37 per cent said yes and 44 per cent said no. Labour voters were still in favour of change by 44 to 36 per cent. This is one of the few opinion polls that has shown more people against than for PR. But it seems to have been a transient mood, encouraged by tabloid coverage of the last few days of the campaign. Voters may be in a more positive frame of mind about the voting system when they have just voted and walked out of the polling station and have not yet heard the result. Polls taken after the election showed that opinion had reverted to normal and there were more people favouring a change to PR than the status quo.

In the aftermath of the election there were attempts to blame the late swing on electoral reform. It is certainly true that there is no point in raising it just to be ambivalent about it or to refuse to give one's point of view. The time for debate and discussion was long before the election. In a campaign people want clear answers. The hint of a change at that late stage of the campaign could easily be interpreted as vacillation or as a cynical attempt to win over Liberal Democrat voters. It was the appearance of being undecided that was damaging. In fact Neil Kinnock had been convinced that electoral reform was inevitable for over four years, although he was unable to say so.

But it is far from clear whether there really was as substantial a late swing against Labour as some pollsters have maintained. The polls may have overestimated Labour support throughout the campaign. And what late swing there was may have been caused by tactical voters realising, as polling day approached, or even at the polling station, that if they wanted a Labour government it was better to vote for a Liberal

Democrat who might beat the Tory than for a Labour candidate who would end up third. In any case, as was argued in Chapter 4, the polls may have reflected opinion more accurately than the election itself.

Among Labour Party members there is an even greater majority for reform. Patrick Seyd and Paul Whiteley found absolutely no reduction in support for electoral reform when they re-interviewed the previous sample of party members after the 1992 election. There were still 58 per cent in favour, but the number who were opposed had gone down from 31 to 29 per cent. New members who had joined the Labour Party in 1991 and 1992 showed even stronger support, with 65 per cent to 21 per cent favouring PR.

12 LET THE PEOPLE DECIDE: FROM 1993

When John Smith took over as Labour leader in July 1992, he was an unknown quantity on electoral reform although he had voted with the Labour government for PR for the European Parliament. Neil Kinnock had been careful not to commit himself while he was leader but by the end of the year he had told David Dimbleby in a television interview that he had been privately convinced for some time of the need for a change in the voting system. By the spring of 1993 he had joined LCER as a sponsor and spoken on an LCER platform at the party's Welsh Conference in Llandudno.

Meanwhile the Plant Commission presented its final report to the National Executive Committee on 19 May 1993, with recommendations on voting systems for elections to the European Parliament, the House of Lords and the House of Commons. On the European Parliament it recommended a regional list system, now on the statute book in the European Parliamentary Elections Act. On a future second chamber it also recommended a regional list PR system. But on elections to the House of Commons there was no majority in favour of a proportional system and the Commission recommended change in the form of the supplementary vote (SV). This system allowing voters to express a first and second choice was put forward in a paper from the Workington MP, Dale Campbell-Savours.

John Smith, however, was not keen on this proposal. He responded to the Plant Report by saying, in effect, that the choice of voting systems for the Commons was too important to be left to politicians. "It is a matter of such constitutional significance that it should be for the people to decide. I firmly believe that the final decision must be taken by means of a referendum ... to be held during the first parliament of the next Labour government ... at a time when the Labour Government had begun the most radical programme of constitutional reform this century."

The main drawback of the SV was that it would not help Labour voters in the south. John Denham, newly elected MP for Southampton Itchen and one of only ten Labour MPs representing the South outside London, showed through a series of computer simulations in his pamphlet, *Electoral Reform and the Regions*, that SV could cost Labour seats in the South but would help the Liberal Democrats in the South-west and might help Labour gain even more seats in Scotland and Wales. He argued: "Where MPs come from is as important as how many each party has." Giles Radice in his Fabian pamphlet, *Southern Discomfort*, drew attention to the party's problems over winning in the South.

John Smith's proposal for a referendum was not in time for the annual round of trade union conferences from April to July. Many trade union leaders and key activists were in favour of electoral reform. Trade union members were largely positive, as Seyd and Whiteley showed in their research in 1992, but conference delegates were less so. There had been no time for unions to consult their branches or their members. The result was that several large unions who might have supported the referendum came out against it. At the TGWU conference on 6 July, there was a knife-edge debate culminating in a speech in favour of PR by Bill Morris, their general secretary. He lost by 19 votes. This meant that the TGWU votes were committed against PR and the referendum.

From the time John Smith offered to let the people decide, attention switched from systems to process, from "would the Labour leader back PR?" to "when and if the referendum would be held". The First Past the Post Campaign was set up in May 1993, with Derek Fatchett MP in the chair. It worked to overturn the referendum pledge. Electoral reform was not in Labour's constitutional proposals, "A new agenda for democracy", presented to that year's annual conference, but the speech of the shadow home secretary, Tony Blair, was an impassioned plea for a new politics. "We cannot renew or rebuild our society, its community or its citizens, unless we first renew its democracy ... What we propose today is a revolution in democratic accountability and control to redistribute power from government to people."

At the conference the referendum proposal was carried, with the

GMB saving the day by supporting the referendum even though they did not support a change in the voting system. When it came to a motion on the voting system, the GMB switched to the other side and a motion supporting FPTP was passed against the platform by 45 to 35 per cent. The Constituency Labour Parties, it should be noted, voted 58 to 42 per cent in favour of electoral reform. The party's internal consultation on the Plant recommendations also showed that 55 per cent of constituencies were in favour. The conference also supported the Plant recommendations for new proportional voting systems for elections to the European Parliament, the new Scottish Parliament and a democratically elected second chamber. For the first time since 1926, a Labour conference had voted for PR, albeit for everything but the Commons.

The debate on electoral reform was not helped by press reporting on the subject, which was often confused and sometimes plain wrong. The decision of the Italian people in a referendum to change their voting system from a national list to an additional member system (AMS) was constantly reported on the BBC as a switch to FPTP. This myth was perpetuated even by the then prime minister. Answering a question from Cheryl Gillan on 22 April 1993, John Major said: "The Italians are right to scrap the backstairs deals that inevitably come from PR." Eventually the BBC had to admit they were wrong and apologise. The Italians were simply introducing a constituency element into a list system, creating the kind of mixed system which the Labour MP Jeff Rooker had championed in the Plant Commission.

The myth about the Italian referendum was repeated by Saatchi and Saatchi in their advertisement for the NO campaign in the New Zealand referendum. They were taken to the Advertising Standards Complaints Board. Despite this misleading propaganda and despite heavy television advertising by the NO campaign, calling itself "The Campaign for Better Government", New Zealanders were more impressed by the arguments of the poorly funded Electoral Reform Coalition and voted by 53.8 per cent to 46.2 per cent to change from FPTP to a system called mixed member proportional (MMP), a variant of AMS, at the same time as their general election, on 6 November 1993.

New Zealand's experience has many lessons for this country as it was as close a parallel as one could hope to find. New Zealand had always used FPTP, but increasing popular discontent with the system had finally led to a "preferendum" in September 1992 when New Zealanders were asked, as the first stage in a two-stage referendum, whether they were in favour of a change in principle and, if so, which system they preferred. The answer was that 85 per cent wanted a change and 70 per cent opted for MMP, the recommendation of their royal commission.

The two referendum campaigns opened up a discussion not only on voting systems but on style of government. As New Zealand's trade union council said in a submission to the electoral commission in 1993: "The vote for change was a call by the people for greater participation and for a political system that informs, involves and empowers the maximum number of people. It was a rejection not only of authoritarian governments but of authoritarian management in the economy and in the workplace."

As a definition of the new politics, this was a good start. Raymond Plant made the same point about his report: "A party which is restating the values of the new politics, common purposes, common identity, social justice and a sense of community cannot be happy with a voting system which is producing a more exclusivist political culture and geographical fragmentation." The same change in political culture was being sought by John Hume, MP, leader of the Social Democratic & Labour Party, who took the initiative that led to the peace talks in Northern Ireland. As he put it: "The basis of democracy is not majority rule but agreement about the way we are governed."

New Zealand and Italy were not the only countries that were changing their voting systems. Japan decided to move to a similar mixed member system but without a referendum. When South Africa was discussing what system to adopt in the first post-apartheid elections, it dismissed FPTP immediately, opting instead for a national list system. Its PR lists ensured that almost a quarter of the National Assembly were women. Since then there has been some discussion of introducing constituencies into this system but not of dropping the principle that seats gained must reflect votes cast. Another shock to supporters of FPTP was the 1994 federal election in Canada which saw the governing Progressive Conservative Party reduced from 167 seats to 2. That sent shudders through the British Conservatives at a time when several MPs were already considering abandoning their marginal seats for safer seats after boundary changes in what came to be known as the "chicken run".

The work of the boundary commissions, which were conducting their now 8–12 yearly review of the boundaries of parliamentary constituencies, was bound to have an effect on the result of the election. The Labour Party took the public inquiries very seriously in order to minimise the inevitable losses that can cost the party up to 20 seats after a boundary review. They paid particular attention to medium-sized towns or cities surrounded by countryside, where the boundary commission has to decide whether to split the town in half and attach each half to a part of the surrounding countryside (a process known as sandwiching) or to draw the constituency tight round the town to produce an entirely urban constituency, known as doughnuting. Sandwiching can often produce two Conservative seats where doughnuting would produce one Labour seat. When the new boundaries were announced in 1995 the projections showed that instead of making a loss of 15 or 20 seats, as it had in previous boundary reviews, the Labour Party might suffer a net loss of only five seats. Colin Rallings and Michael Thrasher, University of Plymouth psephologists, forecast that the Conservatives would gain seven seats, Labour would gain two and the Liberal Democrats would lose two, directly as a result of boundary changes and assuming no change in votes. The effort that the Labour Party had invested in the boundary commissions had paid off.

The Plant Commission was wound up in December 1993 even though its work was still not complete. There was no agreed voting system for a Welsh Assembly, for a Greater London Authority, for English regional assemblies or indeed for local government. In January 1994 Raymond Plant became the LCER's president. The work of the Plant Commission was taken up by the Institute for Public Policy

Research and, when it was established in 1995, by the Constitution Unit directed by Robert Hazell.

The Scottish Labour Party at its 1994 conference in Dundee agreed that: "Labour's commitment to democratic pluralism and a new constitutional settlement for the 21st century will lack credibility without a commitment to change the voting system for the House of Commons." After John Smith's death in May 1994, all three candidates for Labour's leadership supported the referendum, including Tony Blair who wrote at that time: "I fully support the Party's commitment to a referendum on the issue of the electoral system for the House of Commons and existing Party policy for both the European Parliament and an elected second chamber. With regards to an electoral system of a future Scottish Parliament, the Scottish Constitutional Convention has agreed that first past the post is not appropriate. I fully concur with this view."

Tony Blair did not mention the referendum in his first annual conference speech as leader but the conference voted overwhelmingly to confirm its 1993 decision in favour. Later in Glasgow on 11 November, Tony Blair said: "Changing the way we run things is essential if we are to restore people's faith in the democratic process. This is not just reinventing government, it's reinventing politics … a change in the way we govern ourselves." The report of the Borrie Commission on Social Justice pointed out that winner-takes-all electoral systems were said to result in one-party states. Electoral competition should be used to spur good and responsive government.

Two new organisations were set up to campaign for a change in the voting system. The Voting Reform Group brought together supporters of electoral reform from different parties and pressure groups such as Charter 88 and the Electoral Reform Society. Another group calling itself originally 57% Democracy became Democratic Consensus and organised several meetings learning from the Scottish Constitutional Convention and the New Zealand referendum. In April 1995 Labour adopted its new Clause 4 and included the phrase "open democracy". The Joseph Rowntree Reform Trust State of the Nation poll confirmed that the type of question asked on PR makes a difference to the answer.

In the summer of 1995, the Scottish Constitutional Commission presented its report, *Further Steps towards a scheme for Scotland's Parliament*, recommending to the Scottish Constitutional Convention: "a substantial move towards proportionality, sufficient to avoid the 'Westminster' syndrome whereby a party achieving little more than 40 per cent of the vote can routinely win an overall majority of seats".

The debate for and against the referendum was in danger of becoming confused with the debate for and against a change in the voting system. Most people who supported change backed the referendum, even if they disliked referendums on other subjects, whereas most of the people who were in favour of keeping FPTP wanted to ditch the referendum promise. However, in his leader's speech to the 1995 annual conference, Tony Blair recommitted himself to the referendum, saying it gave people "the chance to decide the system by which they elect the government of the future". Jack Straw closed the debate saying: "The right to vote is the most precious right in any democracy; for three decades or more the question of how we vote in this country has been under challenge." So he asked the conference to ensure that John Smith's pledge was reaffirmed. And it was.

Tony Blair's John Smith memorial lecture in February 1996 set the tone for the constitutional input into the *Road to the Manifesto*, Labour's draft manifesto. He spoke of his vision of a new Britain: "a politics in which we are giving power back to the people. A stake in the economy, a stake in society and a stake in the political system." The special "Road to the Manifesto" meeting of the National Policy Forum in June 1996 heard Hilary Benn report back from the workshops on the new politics that a consensus had emerged that the voting referendum should appear in the manifesto. The promise appeared in the long version but not in the summary of *New Labour, new Britain* which Labour members then voted for in the autumn.

One important point that remained undecided was the voting system for election to the Welsh Assembly. Wales had had no equivalent of the Scottish Constitutional Convention but, given the weight of Conservative attacks on the Assembly, a pragmatic decision was to go for symmetry. Tony Blair backed the shadow Welsh Secretary, Ron Davies, in his determination to ensure that the Welsh Assembly would be elected by a similar system to Scotland's AMS. The argument was that FPTP would produce a Labour-dominated Assembly whereas AMS would allow for a Welsh Assembly with Labour as the strongest party and other parties represented in line with votes. On St David's Day, 1 March 1997, the Welsh Labour Party voted at its conference in Llandudno for both a Welsh Assembly and AMS to elect it.

During this time the Labour Party had been having talks with the Liberal Democrats to try to find an agreed programme of constitutional reform which both parties could support. The Joint Consultative Committee on the Constitution, co-chaired by Robin Cook and Robert Maclennan, launched its report on 5 March 1997. At the launch Robin Cook commented: "If this programme is enacted, Britain's democracy will have been transformed. We will enter the 21st century a stronger, more democratic and more open society. It is a prize for which both parties were determined to work." The report's recommendations entered Labour's manifesto, *Because Britain deserves better*, later that month in the section on new politics.

- ♦ We have long supported a proportional system for election to the European Parliament.
- ♦ We are committed to a referendum on the voting system for the House of Commons.
- ♦ An independent commission on voting systems will be appointed early to recommend a proportional alternative to the "first past the post" system.
- ♦ We will enact legislation to allow the people of Scotland and Wales to vote in separate referendums on our proposals (both the Scottish Parliament and the Welsh Assembly to be elected by an additional member system).
- ♦ Following a referendum to confirm popular demand, there will be a new deal for London, with a strategic authority and a mayor, each directly elected.

Although little attention was given to these pledges on "new politics" during the campaign, they were enthusiastically received at local candidate meetings arranged on Charter 88's Democracy Day, 22 April where people spoke of electoral reform in the context of changing centralised, secretive and unrepresentative government. In the early morning of 2 May, Labour was returned with 418 MPs and many of the new MPs were committed to a change in the voting system. So was Martin Bell, the Independent MP for Tatton, who only beat Neil Hamilton, and the FPTP system, because the Labour and Liberal Democrat candidates were withdrawn. When Tony Blair arrived on the steps of 10 Downing Street his message had a special resonance for electoral reformers. He said: "It was a mandate to get those things done in our country that desperately need doing for the future. ... Today, enough of talking. It is time now to do."

So would the new Government push ahead with a change in the voting system that had just given it such a huge majority? Fieldwork carried out in summer 1997 by Patrick Seyd and Paul Whiteley showed remarkably consistent support among Labour members for the proposition that "Britain's present electoral system should be replaced by a system of proportional representation". Previous surveys had been carried out when Labour was in opposition, electoral reform was in the news and the Plant Commission deliberating. However, even after the landslide achieved under the FPTP system, over half, 52 per cent, of those surveyed supported change with only 27 per cent opposed.

Stephen Twigg, who went on to become Chair of the LCER in Spring 1998, summed up the continued commitment to electoral and wider constitutional reform among new Labour MPs when he spoke in the debate on the Queen's Speech on 16 May. He said: "This parliament owes it to our young people to forge a new sort of politics based on consensus, dialogue and cooperation. ... This is not some arcane, abstract debate that is of interest only to the so-called chattering classes. .. . Constitutional reform ... has real relevance to the bread and butter concerns of our constituents. ... It is about devolving power to the people. ... Proportional representation for this

House is an idea whose time has come. Electoral reform is an important democratic change, which will assist in the renewal of hope and faith in politics itself. Labour's proposed referendum will enable the people to decide how the House is elected. It is a momentous and crucial commitment."

The worst fears of some Conservatives had materialised. The system that had given them political domination of the 20th century had dealt them a double blow. Labour had been taught a lesson about 'elective dictatorship' by Margaret Thatcher who had explained to David Frost in June 1995 why the Tories could not afford to lose the general election: "that's crazy – if you went into opposition you may not get back for many years. They might change the voting system".

Constitutional reform, of which voting reform is an integral part, is not about tearing up our history but building on what is good and changing what is not. Labour's victory in May 1997 gave the British people the opportunity and, in the Independent Commission on the voting system and the referendum, the process by which they can decide how they will elect MPs in the future.

13 THE SYSTEM FOR THE FUTURE

Before getting bogged down in detailed arguments about systems (which are explained on page 133), it is as well to stand back and look at the principles which should guide our choice of "an alternative to the present system for the parliamentary elections to be put before the people in the Government's referendum". The terms of reference of the Independent Commission on the Voting System start by saying that they "shall be free to consider and recommend any appropriate system or combination of systems", but they go on to lay down four different, and not necessarily always compatible, criteria for a new voting system. It should observe:

1   the requirement for broad proportionality;
2   the need for stable government;
3   an extension of voter choice; and
4   the maintenance of the link between members and
    geographical constituencies.

These criteria pull in different directions. The "requirement for broad proportionality" seems to be telling the Jenkins Commission to recommend a proportional system, which would restrict their choice to AMS, STV or regional list.

The "need for stable government" begs a question. Does stable government mean a majority government? No system can guarantee stable government, far less effective government. Forecasts of a hung parliament in 1992 under our current system never materialised, but John Major's government, though stable in the sense that it survived, was forced to engage in deals with other parties and unrepresentative elements within his own party.

Many coalition governments have been very stable, but it seems likely that stable government was intended to mean majority government and it is certainly arguable that majority governments are on the whole more stable. If majority government is meant, then they probably reckon that FPTP and AV are the systems most likely to deliver them, though FPTP and AV can produce coalitions and proportional systems can elect majority governments. Spain and Greece elected majority governments throughout the 1970s and 1980s on regional list systems. Sweden has experienced decades of one-party (although rarely majority) government on a regional list system. It should be noted, however, that Greece has sometimes applied a high threshold to its lists system, requiring parties to win up to 17 per cent or even 25 per cent of the vote before they win any seats. Spain has a regional system that tends to exclude a number of small parties.

So all systems are capable of delivering majority government, but proportional systems, such as AMS, STV or regional list, are more likely to deliver it if they are reinforced with high thresholds or other rules that discriminate against small parties, like having to win a seat before qualifying for a top-up in an AMS system. Indeed, it would be quite possible to devise a proportionally-based system that can only result in majority government. In a sense the election of the Greater London Authority will be such a system. But other devices can be found to ensure that an election must result in the election of a government with a majority.

The "maintenance of a link between members and geographical constituencies" limits the choice to a constituency-based system. Only two of the systems on offer have constituency-only single-member systems where all MPs represent a single constituency. They are FPTP and AV. But the Jenkins criteria only say the link should be maintained. They do not say that every MP has to represent a constituency or that every constituency has to have a single MP. AMS has single-member constituencies for the majority of MPs (57 per cent in the new Scottish Parliament and 66 per cent in the Welsh Assembly), but not for all. STV has multi-member constituencies. They exist in local government where three councillors represent the same ward, although STV constituencies for general elections are more likely to have five seats. Only the regional list system has no constituencies, although MPs still represent their regions.

An "extension of voter choice" is the least explicit of the four criteria. Voter choice could be extended in many different directions. It could refer to choice of candidates, choice of parties or choice of government. Some reformers concentrate on choice of candidate and would see STV and perhaps AV as extending choice through preferential voting. But let us assume they are referring to what is generally seen as the main failing of the FPTP system. This is the problem known as wasted votes, or failure to make votes count or give votes an equal value. In the UK, unlike any other European country, most voters go to vote knowing that their individual vote is very unlikely to make any difference to the outcome.

This may be because they are among the one-third of the electorate who do not support either of the parties that are the effective contenders in their constituency and cannot therefore influence the outcome unless they engage in tactical voting. Or it may be because they are among the two-thirds of the electorate who live in seats that are safe for one party or another and the result is a foregone conclusion even when it is a closely fought election in the country at large. These two categories do not account for the entire electorate because they overlap, but the bulk of the parties' energies are focused on less than 15 per cent of the population who live in constituencies on their target list and within those constituencies they will be concentrating their attention on 70,000 swing voters who will decide the outcome of the election. That is less than two voters in every thousand.

Although many people identify lack of *proportionality* as the main problem of our voting system, it is the lack of what might be called *instrumentality* that is far more destructive. Under any other voting system you are more or less guaranteed, if you vote for one of the main parties, that your vote will help to decide what government is elected and will help to elect an MP of your party. But under our system the link is much weaker. Even in 1997, in the year of an electoral landslide, less than 37 per cent of the electorate voted successfully for the candidate who was elected, and less than 31 per cent voted for the new government. That left many voters in many parts of the country feeling that their votes did not count, that they had no leverage on the political system.

Many voters have long since resorted to tactical voting, voting for a party they do not support in order to get rid of a party they like even less. That has now created enormous distortions in voting behaviour across the country. It also creates enormous distortions in the parties' behaviour, explaining their focus on key seats and target voters and also their neglect of non-marginal and non-target voters, which is probably the single most important reason for the low turnout in UK elections. In 1997 Labour scored its biggest election victory after the most focused and targeted campaign in its history and turnout dropped to 71 per cent, the lowest since 1935.

The type of tactical voting we have experienced under FPTP will be resolved by a switch to any other system, including AV, AMS, STV and regional list. Each resolves the problem in a different way. AV can be said to take the blindfold off tactical voting. It allows Labour voters to vote Labour as their first choice and make their tactical vote their second preference. The other systems cure the problem by allowing their vote to count towards the election of a Labour MP elsewhere in a larger constituency or a region. The solution to the second problem, that of wasted votes in safe constituencies, can be achieved by adopting AMS, STV or the regional list system, which all ensure that votes cast for a party large enough to be represented in parliament will count towards the election of an MP wherever it is cast.

So, in summary, if we look at the four criteria in the Commission's terms of reference, proportionality, stable government, the extension of voter choice and the constituency link, and we interpret the voter choice as a need to extend choice to third-party voters and to voters in safe seats, then we can see that, on a simplistic level, there is only one convincing answer to the question that the Commission was asked to investigate. FPTP is, on these criteria, the worst voting system; AV can be an improvement, but a partial one; STV and the regional list do not have the link between a constituency and a single MP; only AMS could potentially satisfy all the criteria, and then only if it were suitably reinforced to facilitate the election of majority governments or minority or partnership governments considered stable.

TABLE 13.1   ANALYSIS OF THE CRITERIA

	FPTP	AV	STV	AMS	List
Proportionality	No	No	Yes	Yes	Yes
Stable government	Yes	Yes	Yes if	Yes if	Yes if
Constituency link	Yes	Yes	No[a]	Yes	No
Extending choice to third parties	No	Yes	Yes	Yes	Yes
Extending choice to safe seats	No	No	Yes	Yes	Yes
Positive score	2	3	3-4	4-5	3-4

a Under STV MPs will have a constituency link but with multi-member constituencies.

So we could leave it there and declare AMS the clear winner on points. But AMS is still flawed in some politicians' eyes because they want a majority government and they fear that AMS will lead to permanent coalition. They will cite the evidence of Germany, which has had AMS since their constitution was drawn up by the Allies after the second world war and has had coalition governments for nearly all that time. They will particularly point to the role of the German Liberal Party, the FPD, which has won only two constituency seats in all of that time but has received sufficient additional seats under the AMS system to hold the balance of power. On the other hand it could be argued that German coalition governments have been very stable despite the change of coalition partners in 1982. There could be a constitutional safeguard in the UK to prevent coalition partners changing without having a general election.

Nowadays, they will also point to the experience in New Zealand which adopted a variant of the AMS system called mixed member proportional (MMP). The parties took several weeks to form a government. Eventually Winston Peters, leader of the small New Zealand First Party which had campaigned as an opponent of the right-wing National Party, switched sides and entered a coalition with them. That was immediately seized upon by opponents of the system as evidence that it would give the power of king-maker to small parties. New Zealand is monitoring its new system but it is unlikely to return to FPTP.

In the past electoral reformers have only been able to discuss the merits of voting systems by reference to experience in other countries. Of the four systems on offer, alternative vote (AV) was usually described as the Australian system; the additional member system (AMS) as the German system; the single transferable vote (STV) as the Irish system, while the regional list was the system used in almost every other European country. But there are not only different systems. One can apply different rules to the same system and even apparently small differences in rules can make a huge difference to the likely outcome of a system.

By the time of the referendum on the voting system for elections to the House of Commons, in 1999 or 2000, there will be first-hand experience of many of these systems in this country. The AMS will be used in the first elections to the Scottish Parliament and the Welsh Assembly in May 1999. A PR regional list system will be used to elect Britain's members of the European Parliament for the first time in June 1999. The supplementary vote (SV) is to be used to elect the first directly elected mayor of London in May 2000 alongside an Assembly elected by AMS. The STV is already used in local elections and European elections in Northern Ireland. It remains to be seen whether this experience of different voting systems within the UK will make people more or less inclined to support a new voting system for the House of Commons.

Before reaching a conclusion we need to consider a broader question about what people are trying to achieve when they vote in elections. In general elections they are exercising three distinct choices.

They are choosing an MP to represent the interests of an area, electing a parliament to reflect the diversity of the nation and picking the best government to run the country for the next five years. The nature of these choices is quite different. The choice of an individual MP is definitive. It tends to become polarised between two candidates and one has to choose one or the other. There is no compromise. The election of a parliament, on the other hand, is non-definitive. There can be as many parties as one likes, mixed in whatever proportions. The choice of government, at least in this country, tends to be definitive. There are only two realistic possibilities. One has to choose between them.

In the UK we make all three choices through a single vote. We try to do this through a very imperfect voting system that has remained largely unchanged since the first parliament of 1265. It evolved as a way of choosing territorial representatives and predates the existence of governments and political parties by several centuries. Yet we now expect this voting system to accomplish tasks for which it was never designed. The way in which we roll these three choices into one is by letting voters choose their MPs, letting MPs choose their party in parliament and then letting the parties determine the choice of government. In practice the voters tend to short-circuit this process by choosing their MPs not for their intrinsic qualities as public representatives but on the basis of their party labels, as an indirect method of choosing the government.

It does not have to be done in this way. In some countries the voter has two votes, one for the MP, another for the party. In Germany, for instance, you can vote for a local MP you happen to like and then vote for a different party in the Bundestag. Your first vote helps to elect your local MP but only your second vote will determine the balance of parties in the Bundestag. In other countries you have two votes: one for your MP, one for the government. In the United States you vote separately for your representative, senator and president. The president then appoints the administration, so when you vote for president, you are in effect choosing your government. In France you also have two elections: one for your MP and the other for your president. The president then appoints a prime minister. In both countries it can result in a president and parliament of different parties. The Americans make a virtue of this, calling it the separation of powers. The French solve the problem by expecting the president of one party to cohabit if necessary with a prime minister of another.

This has very important implications for voting systems. Voting for a single individual, whether an MP or a president, is a definitive choice and can only be accomplished through a majoritarian system, such as FPTP or AV. Voting for a party is an indefinitive choice and can be done more fairly through a proportional system, such as STV or regional list. The reason for the difference lies in the nature of the choice the voters are asked to make. When electing a parliament, assembly or a council, there is a spectrum of possible results, from a majority administration to a hung outcome. When electing a president or a mayor, it can be reduced to a choice between two people. By then there is only one possible result. The election cannot produce a hung president or a hung mayor.

We have seen that it is possible, through AMS, to combine these systems by electing constituency MPs on a majoritarian basis and additional MPs on a proportional basis in such a way that voters have constituency MPs yet their parties are represented proportionately in parliament. It is also possible to elect parliament on a proportional basis and the executive on a majoritarian basis. That is what is likely to happen in the year 2000 when London elects its mayor for the first time. The government's White Paper recommends that the mayor should be elected on a majoritarian basis, SV, and the assembly of 25 should be elected by AMS.

This will be a uniquely British compromise, meeting two of the Jenkins principles of broad proportionality and stable government and preserving a constituency link for the majority of the assembly representatives. It is possible to devise a voting system for the House of Commons which meets all three principles at once. It could determine the choice of both constituency MPs and government through AV and yet, within those parameters, allocate seats to the parties in parliament on a proportionate basis. Voters would just have to mark candidates

and parties in order of preference. Votes would be counted in constituencies, using AV to elect at least half the MPs. The rest would be
elected on a proportional basis as in AMS. Votes would then be aggre-
gated nationally and if a party won more than 50 per cent of the national vote, counting all preferences, it could be guaranteed a working
majority through the additional seats. What one would in effect be
doing is combining a preferential local vote for an MP with a preferential national vote for prime minister, while still allocating seats, as far as
possible within those constraints, on a proportional basis.

In the end the choice is likely to be determined by prosaic considerations. AV and SV are the only new systems that could be introduced without a change in constituency boundaries. The problem for both AMS and
STV is that they would require boundary commissions to sit and report before implementation. This is unrealistic before a 2002 general election. A
new hybrid is being canvassed, AV plus, which is AMS based on AV in single
member constituencies. In order to correct regional disproportionality,
even with AV, there would be an element of proportionality, but to minimise the increase in constituency size there would be fewer additional
members than constituency ones, as for the Scottish Parliament.

This has the intriguing possibility that it could be put on the referendum ballot paper to be implemented in two stages. We would use AV
for the next general election but a positive referendum result would put
the next government under a moral obligation to hold boundary reviews so that the following general election would be held under AMS.

14 VOTING IN THE NEW POLITICS

In the referendum to decide our future voting system, we are bound to hear the argument that constitutional issues are an irrelevance or a sideshow, a diversion from more pressing issues such as health and education that should be our main concern. We will be told that electoral reform is a subject that is never discussed in the pubs and clubs and is of little interest outside the middle-class dinner parties of Islington. But we only have to look at our history to see that constitutional and electoral reform were at the very heart of political debate in the 19th and early 20th centuries, and nowhere more so than in the Labour Party. Did the early socialists not fight for the vote for the working man? Did the infant Labour Party not fight for equal votes for all? Did they have to apologise to their working-class audiences for talking about democratic or constitutional issues? Of course, their listeners understood that equal votes were the key to everything else and were not to be seen as an alternative to trade union rights or social legislation. So now we must reject the craven argument that democratic and constitutional issues are somehow less worthy of our attention than bread-and-butter issues. The reform of our voting system, even though the issues it throws up may sound obscure, is a fundamental issue, easily understood and central to the resolution of many other problems in society.

The great reform movements from the Chartists to the suffragettes fought for the right to vote. But what use is the vote if votes do not count? What good are elections if the result is often a foregone conclusion? A Labour government worthy of its inheritance must grasp the nettle of reform. The fight now is not to win the vote but to ensure that the vote has an equal value for all, wherever we live. People persuade themselves to believe anything that reflects well on themselves, through a process of cognitive delusion. MPs, for instance, can believe

they are elected because they are enormously popular in their constituencies and people vote for them for their personal qualities rather
than their party label. By extension, they can easily convince themselves that the voting system that elected them to parliament is in-
capable of improvement. Some insist that they receive few complaints
and no one raises the issue on the doorstep or in the pub. But the reasons for this are self-evident. MPs spend a lot of time talking to their
own supporters in their own constituencies. By definition these are the
people who have reason to be happy with the system. They voted for
the candidate who won. And if they did not vote for the candidate who
became their MP, they are unlikely to tell him or her so. And if they are
in the pub discussing the failure of the electoral system to deliver the
result they wanted, they are unlikely to do so in front of their MP.

Thus MPs are, almost by definition, the people with least cause for
complaint against the current system and the least likely to hear complaints against it. That is why this Government is determined that the
issue of the voting system should be decided by the voters themselves.
The voting system is the property of the voters, not the politicians, and
the voters must decide. It is not only too important to be left to politicians. It involves their own sectional interests too much to be left to
them. But the result of the referendum can never be final under our un-
written constitution. It is the MPs who will have to vote to change the
system and they are the group that has the clearest interest in the status
quo. When a bill to reform the voting system gets to the floor of the
House of Commons, one can expect it to meet dogged resistance. For
if there is one thing that excites passion among MPs, then it is their own
future. When it comes to the reform of the voting system, the majority of MPs are conservatives.

In view of their vested interest in the voting system, it is remarkable
how many of the new intake of Labour MPs have taken up the cause of
electoral reform. After the general election the Labour Campaign for
Electoral Reform had over 120 sponsors in the House of Commons
and that is by no means a full measure of support for a change in the
voting system. These MPs may have been beneficiaries of the voting

system in 1997 but they recognise that the system is no longer defensible.

The reason why this issue has come to the top of the political agenda is not just that the Labour Party promised a referendum on the voting system, but because of the growing realisation that a high proportion of votes cast under the present system have no effect. Voters might as well use their vote to manipulate the result through tactical voting or to make a political gesture through protest voting or abstain. Defenders of FPTP talk as though the system were static and has always operated in the same way. But if the system has not changed, the voters have. In the 1940s and 1950s they did not question the system. If they supported a party, they voted for the party and that was that. But then the voters began to realise they could operate the system. In hopeless seats many of them started voting tactically or abstaining. The main parties did their best to stop them, but the voters were not stupid. They could see the futility of voting for a party that came a poor third. And it did not escape their notice that the political parties, although they condemned tactical voting, engaged in tactical resourcing, moving as many helpers as they could out of safe and hopeless seats and into marginal seats.

In 1997 many Conservatives experienced for the first time the frustration of finding that their vote did not count. For many Labour voters it was the first time in their lives that their vote had counted. But there were more who, even though Labour was winning nationally, found themselves in seats where Labour came a poor third and a Labour vote was effectively wasted. In all, 221 Labour candidates failed to be elected. Smaller parties have always shared this fate. It is difficult to think of any electoral system that wastes so much time and money to no avail. Nearly all of the resources of the national party campaigns were concentrated on 5 million people living in marginal constituencies. Extra agents, leaders' tours, glossy leaflets, advertising hoardings, all of them were directed at the marginals, who numbered maybe as few as 70,000 swing voters.

Yet what kind of democracy does not value every vote for its own sake? What kind of country does not value all its citizens equally? What kind of party does not value every new supporter without checking nervously whether they live in a marginal constituency or not? Every vote ought to be nurtured and cherished in all its aspects, as an act of citizenship, as an exercise of power, however slight, as a profession of faith and as a commitment to the society in which we live. Voting is about ownership of government. Voting is the means by which the voters exercise their authority over the state. It seems very careless of us to allow this right to vary so arbitrarily in its effects from one con-stituency to another. It seems cavalier to palm off the many permanent minorities trapped within the present voting system, the Labour vot-ers in Somerset and Surrey, or the Conservatives in Leeds and Mersey-side, with the excuse that their views will be represented by like-minded people in other areas.

In the 1997 general election, Labour won eight seats in Kent, but it is worth remembering that in 1992 Labour won 223,225 votes in Kent without winning a single MP – more votes than were necessary to elect all 11 Labour MPs in Glasgow. This left nearly 250,000 voters without any direct say on issues that affected them. On the Channel Tunnel or naval dockyards or cross-channel ferries, their views could only be articulated by northern Labour MPs or by their own Conserv-ative MPs breaking ranks. This dilemma now faces Conservative voters in Scotland and Wales. How can their concerns by addressed when they have no representation whatsoever?

The fundamental issue at the heart of the debate about electoral re-form is simple: is it plausible for a reforming party like the Labour Party to hang on to a creaking, antiquated voting system which runs not only against its long-term interest but also against its commitment to democracy, justice and equality? People deserve a system that reflects the diversity and pluralism of the society we live in and allows all voices to be heard in every forum where decisions are made.

Electoral reform is not an end in itself, it is about changing political culture. The way parliament works is being modernised. The gender balance is slowly creeping in the right direction. But the winner-takes-all attitude remains as long as we keep the present voting system. Today's politics is too often "put up or shut up", confrontational and often mindlessly predictable to those who are not on the inside. Cooperation is not rewarded and adversarial point-scoring often is.

Problem-solving is difficult if each party has to be right or wrong and certain issues are too difficult to talk about. If we want to say "That's brilliant, but have you thought of…" or "Thank you for thinking of that, but what about…?" this is thought of as sycophancy instead of as constructive engagement in the future. Acknowledging that we have not got the answers is weakness; and commissions and consultation, or trying things out in pilot projects, are seen as delaying tactics at best or camouflage for splits in parties. We need a politics where politicians can be honest without losing votes; where their role is to explain rather than defend a course of action and to bring more and more people into the conversation. We need an approach which says we can agree about some things and agree to disagree about others, recognising that difference is natural. We have different experience with differing skills, knowledge and ability; society works best when all its voices are heard and listened to.

Jeff Rooker MP, one of the leading advocates of electoral reform in the Labour Party, identified the issue long ago as one of trust. "The magic ingredient which has been missing for so long is trust. Even with the trauma of the poll tax and the National Health Service cuts, Middle England did not trust Labour. The message we send out by supporting electoral reform is that we recognise that the old way of winner-takes-all on a minority of the votes and then works only for its people is not the way to rebuild our nation."

In any case, is it plausible for a Labour government to pass the Bill of Rights, to reform the House of Lords, to set up new parliaments and assemblies in Scotland, Wales, London and the English regions, to introduce freedom of information legislation, to overhaul the entire constitution without changing the voting system? This would be like a farmer buying the latest technology in combine harvesters, but still pulling it with a cart-horse. The voting system is the part of the constitution most in need of replacement. It is an integral part of a new constitutional settlement. FPTP may have served reasonably well at one time. It may still have a nostalgic appeal for some. But, like the cart-horse, it is best left to graze in the meadow.

The world has changed since the last century when our electoral system developed. It has changed since the heyday of the two-party system in the 1950s. We now live in a pluralist society where many more voices want to be heard. We also live in a consumer society where voters want a wider choice. We want more influence on decisions that affect our lives. Above all we want our votes to count.

The task now is to give the FPTP system a decent burial and present the electorate with a vision of the future that includes a voting system that reflects their aspirations, a system that values every vote in every part of the country. The right to vote was not so lightly won that we can stand by and let the voting system render it useless.

Politics is moving away from the old adversarial courtroom style and trying to find a new way of working, finding consensus rather than conflict, problem-solving rather than point-scoring, getting things done rather than merely stating one's view, looking for common ground and common interest rather than sticking in tribes and thriving on hatred. The midwife for this will be a change in the voting system.

The sceptics have always said that no party elected to power will ever vote to change the voting system that brought them to power. The challenge is to prove them wrong: to show that a party can reach beyond its narrowly perceived vested interest to a greater good. Politics needs to change and a change in the voting system is the necessary catalyst. 1945 was the time of "We are the masters now", and the creation of the welfare state. By 1997, Labour politicians realised that they must be servants of the people and take the opportunity to create the democratic state. At the end of the 20th century a government with the biggest majority for 60 years can break the logjam of old constitutional ideas. The referendum will start the process of building trust and connecting the politicians and the people.

APPENDICES

VOTING SYSTEMS

Additional Member System (AMS)

The name for any mixed system where half or most MPs are elected in constituencies, usually by FPTP although it could be AV or SV, but the overall result is broadly related to votes cast for parties by giving them top-up additional members. If a party wins 20 per cent of the seats but 30 per cent of the vote, it will be given additional MPs to compensate. The result is that nearly everyone has an MP of their own party, either in their constituency or in their region. Different forms of AMS are used in Germany, Italy, Japan and New Zealand. It was recommended for the UK by the Hansard Society in 1976 and by the Institute for Public Policy Research in 1991. Elections to the Scottish Parliament and Welsh Assembly in 1999 and to the London Assembly after the London referendum will all be conducted using an AMS system. It is many Labour reformers' preferred system and is supported by the Green Party, Plaid Cymru and the Scottish Nationalists.

Alternative vote (AV)

Preference voting in single-member constituencies. The ballot paper is as it is at present. Voters may mark the paper 1, 2, 3, etc, in their order of preference. All first choices are counted and if no one has a majority the candidate with the fewest votes drops out and those papers are passed to other candidates according to second preferences. This process is repeated until one candidate has a majority of the votes, at over 50 per cent. Used in the Australian House of Representatives. Supported by Labour's Keep the Link group, in "The Blair Revolution" by Peter Mandelson, and by Roger Liddle and Peter Hain in "Proportional Misrepresentation". John Curtice and the Democratic Audit both projected more disproportionate results in 1997 than under our present system. AV does remove the blindfold from tactical voting but it does not change the results in the heartlands.

AV plus

A new hybrid system being canvassed which is really AMS based on AV in constituencies. If it was the recommendation of the commission then it could be put on the referendum ballot paper to be implemented in two stages. We would use AV for the next election but a positive referendum result would put the next government under a moral obligation to hold boundary commissions and the next but one general election would use AMS or MMS based on slightly larger constituencies with additional members added to correct any imbalance between seats and votes.

First-past-the-post (FPTP)

The present plurality system. Each MP is elected in a single-member constituency. The voter marks the paper with an x. The candidate with more votes than any other candidate wins irrespective of the percentage of votes cast. Used in the UK to elect MPs to the House of Commons and in England, Scotland and Wales to elect local authorities. Also used in Canada, the United States and India.

Mixed member proportional (MMP)

The name given to AMS in New Zealand where it was used for the first time in their 1996 general election. It was introduced after two referendums were held in 1992 and 1993. It comes up for reassessment after the second election in 1999. The constituencies are topped up from national rather than regional lists.

Mixed member system (MMS)

A minimalist AMS specifically designed to overcome most of the objections to reform from Labour supporters of FPTP. There are 500 single-member constituencies and 150 regional members (approximately 75 per cent of constituency MPs and 25 per cent regional). To gain additional members a party has to win one constituency. It gained the support of several reformers on the Plant Commission, including Raymond Plant.

Regional list
People vote for candidates on lists in multi-member constituencies, usually regions in large countries and national lists in smaller ones. If a party gets a quarter of the vote, it gets a quarter of the seats. Parties that get less than the threshold, often 4 or 5 per cent, get no seats at all. Lists can be democratically nominated, selected and ordered by local party members. Voters either select a team of candidates in a fixed or ordered list as nominated, sometimes called closed, or can re-order the list by indicating preference(s) or by deletion. This system encourages parties to present a balanced ticket. It is used in Scandinavia and most countries use the system for elections to the European Parliament. National lists were used in the first South African elections in 1994.

Second ballot (SB)
Precisely the same as FPTP, in single-member constituencies, but if no candidate wins more than 50 per cent of the votes in the constituency, the top two contest the second round one or two weeks later. Used in France.

Single transferable vote (STV)
Preference voting in multi-member constituencies. The voter marks the paper 1, 2, 3, etc, in the order of preference, allowing voters to choose between candidates for the same party as well as choosing between parties themselves. Votes are transferred, as lowest-placed candidates are excluded, as are the surplus votes of candidates who are elected. Candidates have to reach a quota which is the number of voters divided by the number of representatives to be elected plus one. In a five-member seat each party can put up five candidates and votes can vote for all five, though they must put them in order. They can also put the candidates of the other parties in order. Their vote will count only once – for the candidate who needs it – and this usually makes the system proportional. The system is used in Ireland, the Australian Senate, the Lower House in Tasmania and in Northern Ireland for elections to the European Parliament and district councils. It is supported by the

Liberal Democrats and the Electoral Reform Society. It was ruled out by the Plant Commission for lack of monotonicity, a word meaning you cannot harm the chances of your candidate winning by voting for them. A hybrid STV and AV system is being canvassed with AV being used in large but sparsely populated single-member constituencies. It is similar to the one which was almost adopted in 1918.

Supplementary vote (SV)

Retains single-member constituencies and is a cross between AV and the second ballot. Ballot papers are almost the same as in FPTP, except that there are two columns. The voters mark an x against their first-preference candidate. If voters wish they may also place an x, in the second column, against the name of a second-preference candidate. Any candidate with more than 50 per cent of first preferences is elected. If no candidate receives over half the votes, all but the top two candidates are eliminated. The remaining candidate with the most first and second preferences is elected. This system was invented by Dale Campbell-Savours, MP, to overcome problems under the alternative vote, of counting 3rd, 4th, 5th and even lower preferences equally with first preferences. A similar system is used in Sri Lankan presidential elections. It was the recommendation for the House of Commons of the Plant Commission in 1993 and it will be used for the first time to choose London's first directly elected mayor.

READING

Paul Addison, "By-elections of the Second World War", in Chris Cook and John Ramsden (eds): *By-elections in British politics*, Macmillan, 1973, UCL, 1997

Andrew Adonis, *Voting in Proportion: Electoral Reform for Scotland's Councils*, Scottish Council Foundation, 1998

Robert Alexander, *The Voice of the People: A Constitution for Tomorrow*, Weidenfeld & Nicolson, 1997

Graham Allen, *Reinventing Democracy: Labour's mission for the new century*, Features Unlimited, 1995

Douglas J Amy, *Real Choices/New Voices: The Case for Proportional Representation Elections in the United States*, Columbia University Press, New York, 1993

Douglas J Amy, *Proportional Representation: The Case for a Better Election System*, Crescent Street Press, Northampton, Massachusetts, 1997

Paul Anderson and Nyta Mann, *Safety First: The Making of New Labour*, Granta Books, 1997

Lynne Armstrong and Mary Georghiou, *Voting in Europe*, LCER, 1992

Anthony Barnett, *This Time: Our Constitutional Revolution*, Vintage, 1997

Robert Blackburn, *The Electoral System in Britain*, Macmillan, 1995

David Beetham, "Choose Democracy", *New Socialist*, May 1987

David Beetham (ed), *Defining and Measuring Democracy*, Sage, 1994

David Beetham, "The Plant Report and the Theory of Political Representation", *Political Quarterly*, October–December 1992

Tony Benn and Andrew Hood, *Common Sense*, Hutchinson, 1993

Vernon Bogdanor and David Butler (eds), *Democracy and elections: Electoral systems and their political consequences*, Cambridge University Press, 1983

Vernon Bogdanor, *Power and the People: A guide to constitutional reform*, Victor Gollancz, 1997

Ian Budge, *The Challenge of Direct Democracy*, Polity Press, 1996

Richard Burden and Mary Southcott, "2001 – an electoral reform odyssey", *Chartist*, July–August 1997

David Butler and Austin Ranney (eds), *Referendums around the World: The Growing Use of Direct Democracy*, The AEI Press, Washington, 1994

David Butler and Iain Maclean (eds), *Fixing the Boundaries*, Dartmouth, 1996

David Butler and David Kavanagh, *The British General Election of 1997*, Macmillan, 1997

David Butler, *The Case for an Electoral Commission: Keeping election law up-to-date*, King-Hall Paper No 5, The Hansard Society for Parliamentary Government, 1998

Brian Cathcart, *Were you still up for Portillo?*, Penguin Books, 1997

Helena Catt, Ann Christina, Mary Georghiou and Moira Montieth, *Votes for Women, the 'New Suffragettes'*, LCER, 1990

Helena Catt, "The Intelligent Person's Guide to Electoral Reform", *New Statesman and Society*, June 1990

Helena Catt, Paul Harris and Nigel S. Roberts, *Voter's Choice, Electoral Change in New Zealand*, The Dunmore Press, New Zealand, 1992

Charter 88, *The Alternative Vote and UK General Elections 1983–1997*, 1997

Linda Colley, "The illusion of a two-party state", *The Independent*, 28 October, 1992

Linda Colley, "Britain must move with the times to be great again", Channel 4 lecture, Opinions, *The Times*, 8 March, 1993

Commission on Electoral Reform, the Report of the Hansard Society, June 1976, republished in February 1998 with an updating preface by Lord Blake, Chairman of the Commission

Commission on Social Justice, *Social Justice: Strategies for National Renewal*, IPPR/Vintage, 1994

Commission for Local Democracy, *Taking Charge: The Rebirth of Local Democracy*, 1995

Commission on the Conduct of Referendums, *Report of the Commission on the Conduct of Referendums*, The Constitution Unit and Electoral Reform Society, 1996

The Constitution Unit Briefing, *Changing the Electoral System*, March 1997

The Constitution Unit, *Regional Government in England*, 1996

The Constitution Unit, *Reform of the House of Lords*, 1996

Curriculum Guidance Eight, *Education for Citizenship*, National Curriculum Council, 1990

Nigel Currie and Mary Georghiou, *Voices for Change, Lessons from Local Government*, LCER, 1991

John Curtice and Michael Steed, *Proportionality and exaggeration in the British Electoral System*, Electoral Studies, Butterworth-Heinemann, 1986

John Curtice, "The British electoral system: a fixture without foundation", in Dennis Kavanagh (ed), *Electoral Politics*, Clarendon Press, 1992

John Curtice, "The hidden surprise: the electoral system in 1992", *Parliamentary Affairs*, 1992

John Curtice and Michael Steed, "The Results Analysed", in David Butler and David Kavanagh, *The British General Election of 1992*, Macmillan, 1992

John Curtice and Michael Steed, "The Results Analysed", David Butler and David Kavanagh, *The British General Election of 1997*, Macmillan, 1997

F.W.S.Craig, *British Electoral Facts, 1832–1987*, Parliamentary Research Services, 1989, 5th Edition

David Denver and Gordon Hands, "Constituency Campaigning", *Parliamentary Affairs*, October 1992

Michael Dummett, "Toward a More Representative Voting System: The Plant Report", *New Left Review 194*, August 1992

Michael Dummett, *Principles of Electoral Reform*, Oxford University

Press, 1997

Maria Eagle and Joni Lovenduski, *High Time or High Tide for Labour women?*, The Fabian Society, 1998

David M Farrell, *Comparing Electoral Systems*, Prentice Hall Harvester Wheatsheaf, 1997

Alan Francis, *New Votes for Europe: Making the Changes Work for Everyone*, Green Research & Development Trust and Third Wave, 1997

John Garrett, *Westminster, does parliament work?*, Victor Gollancz, 1992

Mary Georghiou and Martin Linton, *Arguments for Electoral Reform*, LCER, 1990, 1991 and 1992

The Guardian Guide to The House of Commons, New Parliament, Martin Linton (ed), Fourth Estate, 1992

Peter Hain, *Proportional Mis-representation: the case against PR in Britain*, Wildwood House, 1986

David Halpern, Stewart Wood, Stuart White & Gavin Cameron (eds), *Options for Britain: A Strategic Policy Review*, Dartmouth, 1996

The Hansard Society Report, *The Public Realm, Women at the Top*, 1990

Jenifer Hart, *Proportional Representation: Critics of the British Electoral System 1820–1945*, Clarendon Press, Oxford, 1992

Anthony Heath, John Curtice, Geoff Evans, Roger Jowell, Julia Field, Sharon Witherspoon: *Understanding Political Change, The British Voter 1964–1987*, Pergamon Press, 1991

Anthony Heath, Roger Jowell and John Curtice with Bridget Taylor (eds), *Labour's Last Chance? The 1992 Election and Beyond*, Dartmouth, 1994

Eric Heffer, *Never a Yes Man,* Verso, 1991

David Held: *Models of Democracy*, Polity Press, 1987, 2nd Edition 1996

Peter Hennessy, *The Hidden Wiring*, Gollancz, 1995

Colin Hughes and Patrick Wintour, *Labour Rebuilt, The New Model Labour Party*, Fourth Estate, 1990

Will Hutton, *The State We're In*, Jonathan Cape, 1995, Vintage, 1996

Will Hutton, *The State To Come*, Vintage, 1997

Institute for Public Policy Research, *The Constitution of the United Kingdom*, 1991

Simon Jenkins, *Accountable to None: the Tory Nationalisation of Britain*, Penguin Books, 1995

Ron Johnston, Charles Pattie and J.G.Allsopp, *A Nation Dividing? The Electoral Map of Great Britain, 1979–1987*, Longman, 1988

Ron Johnston and Charles Pattie, "The changing electoral geography of Great Britain", in David Denver and Gordon Hands, *Issues & Controversies in British Electoral Behaviour*, Harvester Wheatsheaf, 1992

Ron Johnston, Charles Pattie and David Rossiter, "Votes that Count and Votes that Don't: The British Electoral System and the British Electorate", in Danny Dorling and Ludi Simpson: *Demystifying Statistics*, Arnold, 1998

Ron Johnston, Charles Pattie, David Rossiter, Danny Dorling, Iain MacAllister and Helena Tunstall, "Changing Biases in the Operation of the UK's Electoral System, 1950–1997", *British Journal of Politics and International Relations*, Vol 1, 1999

Nicholas Jones, *Election, The Inside Story of the Campaign*, BBC Books, 1992

Nicholas Jones, *Campaign 1997: How the General Election was Won and Lost*, Indigo, 1997

Dennis Kavanagh, *Election Campaigning: The New Marketing of Politics*, Blackwell, 1995

Peter Kellner, "1992 – Why the Tories Won", in *The BBC-Vacher's Guide to the New House of Commons*, 1992

M. Kendall and A. Stuart, "The Law of Cubic Proportions in Election Results", *British Journal of Sociology* I, 1950

Martin Kettle, "Which voters count?", *The Guardian*, 8 February, 1997

Martin Kettle, "Strike first, fast and forget most voters", *The Guardian*, 18 March, 1997

Anthony King (ed), *New Labour Triumphs: Britain at the Polls*, Chatham House, New Jersey, 1997

Richard Kuper, *Electing for Democracy, Proportional Representation and the Left*, Socialist Society, 1990

Labour Campaign for Electoral Reform Newsletter, LCER, 1990–1998

Labour Coordinating Committee, Policy Paper, *Getting it in Proportion – A new electoral system that Labour can support*, LCC, 1990

Arend Lijphart, *Democracies: Patterns of Majoritarian and Consensus Government in Twenty-One Countries*, Yale University Press, 1984

Martin Linton, *Labour Can Still Win*, The Fabian Society, 1988

Martin Linton and Mary Georghiou, "A British Additional Member System? Issues that need to be decided in an AMS system", LCER, 1992

Martin Linton and Mary Georghiou, *Labour's Road to Electoral Reform: what's wrong with first-past-the-post?*, LCER, 1993

Martin Linton, *Money and Votes*, IPPR, 1994

Martin Linton, *Was it the Sun Wot Won it?*, Oxford/Nuffield College, 1995

Martin Linton (ed), *The Election: A Voters' Guide*, A Guardian Book, Fourth Estate, 1997

Ruth Lister, *Citizenship: Feminist Perspectives*, Macmillan, 1997

Adam Lively, *Parliament: The Great British Swindle*, Chatto Counterblasts No 15, Chatto and Windus, 1990

Iain McLean, "Forms of Representation and Systems of Voting", David Held (ed), *Political Theory Today*, Polity Press, 1991

James McCormick and Mary Southcott, *What the Tories fear most*, LCER, 1997

Peter Mair, "The Question of Electoral Reform", *New Left Review 194*, August 1992

Andrew Marr, *Ruling Britannia: The Failure and Future of British Democracy*, Michael Joseph, 1995

Andrew Marr, *The Battle for Scotland*, Penguin Books, 1992

David Marquand and Anthony Seldon, (eds), *The Ideas That Shaped Post-War Britain*, Fontana Press, 1996

Kirsty Milne, "PR: the Piecemeal Revolution", *New Statesman*, 31 October, 1997

Mo Mowlam and Charlette Atkins, "Will Electoral Reform work for women?", *Chartist*, March/April, 1993, LCER, 1993

Beryl Nicholson, "From Interest Group to (Almost) Equal Citizenship: Women's Representation in the Norwegian Parliament", *Parliamentary Affairs*, April 1993

Pippa Norris, Elizabeth Vallance and Joni Lovenduski, "Do Candidates Make a Difference? Gender, Race, Ideology and Incumbency", *Parliamentary Affairs*, October 1992

Pippa Norris & Joni Lovenduski, *Political Recruitment, Gender Race and Class in the British Parliament*, Cambridge University Press, 1995

Pippa Norris and Neil T. Gavin (eds), *Britain Votes 1997*, OUP/Hansard Society, 1997 first published in *Parliamentary Affairs*, 1997

Henry Pelling, *A Short History of the Labour Party*, Macmillan, 1991

Martin Pugh, *The Evolution of the British Electoral System 1832–1887*, The Historical Association, London, 1988

Colin Rallings and Michael Thrasher (compilers and eds), *Media Guide to the New Parliamentary Constituencies*, the Local Government Chronicle Elections Centre for BBC, ITN, the Press Association and Sky News, 1995

Gordon Reece, *How People Vote*, Anthony Wigram, 1983

Gordon Reece, *Voter Representation: A Study of the British Electoral System and its Consequences*, Conservative Action for Electoral Reform, 1995

Andrew Reeve and Alan Ware, *Electoral Systems*, Routledge, 1992

David A J Richards, *Toleration and the Constitution*, Oxford University Press, 1986

Jeff Rooker, *Beaten by the Boundaries*, LCER, 1989

Samizdat on Electoral Reform, Number 12, September/October 1990

Samizdat: Number 16, "Let a Thousand Plants Bloom, Voting Systems", October/November 1991

G.R.Searle, *The Liberal Party: Triumph and Disintegration, 1886–1929*, Macmillan, 1992

David Seymour, "Get Practical", *The Mirror*, 30 April 1997

Patrick Seyd and Paul Whiteley, *Labour's Grass Roots: The Politics of Party Membership*, OUP, 1992

Clare Short, "Promoting pluralism", in *Fabian Conference News Special*, Alison Ryan (ed), September/October 1992

The Sheffield Group, (Editors Pete Alcock, Andrew Gamble, Ian Gough, Phil Lee and Alan Walker), *The Social Economy and the Democratic State*, Lawrence and Wishart, 1989

Jeremy Smith and Iain McLean: *The UK Poll Tax and the Declining Electoral Roll: Unintended Consequences?* No. 398, Warwick Economic Research Papers, Department of Economics, University of Warwick, Coventry, October 1992

Mary Southcott, "Will Labour Change the Way We Vote?", *Liberator*, June 1997

Mary Southcott and Deborah Pate, "A sustainable democracy", *New Ground 52*, SERA, Autumn 1997

Michael Steed, "The Liberal Party", in Henry Drucker: *Multi-Party Britain*, Macmillan, 1979

Mary-Ann Stephenson, *The Glass Trapdoor: Women, politics and the media during the 1997 general election*, Fawcett, 1998

John Stewart, Innovation in Democratic Practice, Inlogov, Institute of Local Government Studies, 1995

Philip Temple, *Making Your Vote Count: referendum 1992: a guide to electoral reform*, John McIndoe, New Zealand, 1992

Philip Temple, *Making Your Vote Count Twice: referendum 1993: MMP vs FPP*, John McIndoe, New Zealand, 1993

Philip Temple, *Much More Passion? MMP One Year On*, Hocken Library, University of Otago, New Zealand

The Times Guide to the House of Commons, April 1992, Times Books, Edited by Alan H Wood and Roger Wood, 1992

The Times Guide to the House of Commons, May 1997, Times Books, Edited by Tim Austin, 1997

Stephen Tindale (ed), *The State and the Nations: The Politics of Devolution*, Institute for Public Policy Research, 1996

Stephen Twigg & Andrew Adonis, *The Cross We Bear*, Fabian Society, 1997

Robert Waller and Byron Criddle, *The Almanac of British Politics*, fifth edition, Routledge, 1996

Stuart Weir, "Waiting for Change: Public Opinion and Electoral Reform", *Political Quarterly*, April–June 1992

Paul Whiteley, Patrick Seyd and Jeremy Richardson, *True Blues: the politics of Conservative Party membership*, OUP, 1994

Tony Wright, *Citizens & Subjects: an essay on British politics*, Routledge, 1994

Tony Wright, *Why Vote Labour?*, Penguin Books, 1997

and

The Plant Reports

Democracy, Representation and Elections, First Interim Report of the Labour Party Working Party on Electoral Systems, Labour Party, 1991

Second Interim Report of the Working Party on Electoral Systems, Labour Party, 1992

Report of the Working Party on Electoral Systems, Labour Party, 1993

representation: journal of representative democracy, published by the McDougall Trust, 1995–

LCER Literature and Newsletters

USEFUL ADDRESSES

The Labour Campaign for
Electoral Reform (LCER)
Butts Cottage, The Butts,
Rodborough, Stroud. GL5 3TZ
Tel 01453 756649
and 0117 924 5139

The Advisory Group for the
Teaching of Citizenship and
Democracy in Schools
c/o Qualifications and
Curriculum Authority,
Newcombe House,
45 Notting Hill Gate,
London. W11 3JB
Tel 0171 243 9365

Charter 88
(campaign for a modern
and fair democracy)
Exmouth House,
3–11 Pine Street,
London. EC1R 0JH
Tel 0171 833 1988

The Democratic Left
6 Cynthia Street,
London. N1 9JF
Tel 0171 278 4443

Make Votes Count
(YES Campaign in the
Referendum on changing the
voting system)
PO Box 23129,
London. SE1 0ZR
Tel 0171 928 2076

Electoral Reform Society
5 Chancel Street,
London. SW1 0UU
Tel 0171 928 1622

Fabian Society
11 Dartmouth Street,
London. SW1H 9BN
Tel 0171 222 8877

Fawcett Society
45 Beech Street,
London. EC2Y 8AD
Tel 0171 628 2865

Friends of the Earth
26 Underwood Street,
London. N1 7JT
Tel 0171 490 1555

Conservative Party
32 Smith Square,
London. SW1P 3HH
Tel 0171 222 9000

Green Party
1a Waterlow Road,
London. N19 5NJ
Tel 0171 272 4474

Labour Party
Millbank Tower,
Millbank,
London. SW1P 4GT
Tel 0171 802 1000

Liberal Democrats
4 Cowley Street,
London. SW1P 3NB
Tel 0171 222 7999

Plaid Cymru
18 Park Grove,
Cardiff. CF1 3BN
Tel 01222 646000

Scottish National Party
6 North Charlotte Street,
Edinburgh. EH2 4JH
Tel 0131 226 3661

Sinn Fein
5 Conway Street,
Belfast. BT13 2DA
Tel 01232 230261

Social Democratic &
Labour Party
Cranmore House,
121 Ormeau Road,
Belfast. BT7 1SH
Tel 01232 247700

Socialist Labour Party
9 Victoria Road,
Barnsley. S70 2BB
Tel 01226 770957

Ulster Democratic Unionist
91 Dundela Avenue,
Belfast. BT4 3BU
Tel 01232 471155

Ulster Unionist Party
3 Glengall Street,
Belfast. BT12 5AE
Tel 01232 324601

20TH-CENTURY UK ELECTIONS

Date	Party	Votes	% vote	% seats	Seats
	Con	1,767,958	50.3	60.0	402
1900	Lab	62,698	1.3	0.3	2
	Lib	1,572,323	45.0	27.3	183
	Con	2,422,071	43.4	23.3	156
1906	Lab	321,663	4.8	4.3	29
	Lib	2,751,057	49.4	59.6	399
	Con	3,104,407	46.8	40.6	272
1910	Lab	505,657	7.0	6.0	40
Jan	Lib	2,866,157	43.5	40.9	274
	Con	2,420,169	46.6	40.4	271
1910	Lab	371,802	6.4	6.3	42
Dec	Lib	2,293,869	44.2	40.6	272

WARTIME COALITION 1916–18

Date	Party	Votes	% vote	% seats	Seats
	Con	5,121,359	47.6	67.6	478
1918	Lab	2,385,472	22.2	8.9	63
	Lib	1,298,808	12.1	4.0	28
	Con	5,502,298	38.5	55.9	344
1922	Lab	4,237,349	29.7	23.1	142
	Lib	2,668,143	18.9	10.1	62
	NatLib	1,471,317	9.9	8.6	53

Total	*Women MPs*	*Type of government*	*Labour leader*
670		Con majority 134	
670		Lib majority 128	Keir Hardie (1906)
670		Minority Lib government	Arthur Henderson (1908) George Barnes (1910)
670		Minority Lib government	Ramsay MacDonald (1911) Arthur Henderson (1914)
707	0 0 0+1a	Con Coalition majority 249	William Adamson (1917) Jimmy Clynes (1921)
615	1 0 1 0	Con majority 73	Ramsay MacDonald (1922)

Date	Party	Votes	% vote	% seats	Seats
	Con	5,514,541	38.0	42.0	258
1923	Lab	4,439,780	30.7	31.1	191
	Lib	4,301,481	29.7	25.7	158
	Con	7,854,523	46.8	67.0	412
1924	Lab	5,489,087	33.3	24.6	151
	Lib	2,928,737	17.8	6.5	40
	Con	8,656,225	38.1	42.3	260
1929	Lab	8,370,417	37.1	46.7	287
	Lib	5,308,738	23.5	9.6	59
	Nat	14,529,385	67.2	90.1	554
1931	Lab	6,649,630	30.9	8.5	52
	Ind Lib	103,528	0.5	0.7	4
	Nat/Con	11,755,654	53.3	69.8	429
1935	Lab	8,325,491	38.0	25.0	154
	Ind Lib	1,443,093	6.7	3.4	21

WARTIME COALITION 1940–1945

	Con	9,972,010	39.6	32.8	210
1945	Lab	11,967,746	48.0	61.4	393
	Lib	2,252,430	9.0	1.9	12
	Con	12,492,404	43.4	47.7	298
1950	Lab	13,266,176	46.1	50.4	315
	Lib	2,621,487	9.1	1.4	9

Total	Women MPs	Type of government	Labour leader
615	3	Minority	
	3	Lab government	
	2		
615	3	Con	
	1	majority 209	
	0		
615	3	Minority	
	9	Lab government	
	1		
615	13	National	Arthur Henderson
	0	majority of 493	(1931)
	1+1a		George Lansbury
			(1932)
615	6	Con	
	1	and National	Clement Attlee
	1+1a	majority 243	(1935)
640	1	Lab	
	21	majority 146	
	1+1a		
625	6	Lab	
	14	majority 5	
	1		

Date	Party	Votes	% vote	% seats	Seats
	Con	13,718,199	48.0	51.4	321
1951	Lab	13,948,883	48.8	47.2	295
	Lib	730,546	2.6	1.0	6
	Con	13,310,891	49.7	54.8	345
1955	Lab	12,405,254	46.4	44.0	277
	Lib	722,402	2.7	1.0	6
	Con	13,750,875	49.4	57.9	365
1959	Lab	12,216,172	43.8	41.0	258
	Lib	1,640,760	5.9	1.0	6
	Con	12,002,642	43.4	48.3	304
1964	Lab	12,205,808	44.1	50.3	317
	Lib	3,099,283	11.2	1.4	9
	Con	11,418,455	41.9	40.2	253
1966	Lab	13,096,629	48.0	57.8	364
	Lib	2,327,457	8.6	1.9	12
	Con	13,145,123	46.4	52.4	330
1970	Lab	12,208,758	43.1	45.7	288
	Lib	2,117,035	7.5	1.0	6
	Con	11,872,180	37.9	46.8	297
1974	Lab	11,645,616	37.2	47.4	301
Feb	Lib	6,059,519	19.3	2.0	14
	Con	10,462,565	35.8	43.6	277
1974	Lab	11,457,079	39.2	50.2	319
Oct	Lib	5,346,704	18.3	2.0	13

Total	Women MPs	Type of government	Labour leader
625	6	Con	
	11	majority 17	
	0		
630	10	Con	Hugh Gaitskell
	14	majority 60	(1955)
	0		
630	12	Con	Harold Wilson
	13	majority 100	(1963)
	0		
630	11	Lab	
	18	majority 4	
	0		
630	7	Lab	
	19	majority 98	
	0		
630	15	Con	
	10	majority 30	
	0+1[a]		
635	9	Minority	
	13	Lab government	
	0+1[a]		
635	7	Lab	
	18	majority 3	James Callaghan
	0+2[a]		(1976)

Date	Party	Votes	% vote	% seats	Seats
	Con	13,697,923	43.9	53.4	339
1979	Lab	11,532,218	36.9	42.4	269
	Lib	4,313,804	13.8	1.7	11
	Con	13,012,316	42.4	61.1	397
1983	Lab	8,456,934	27.6	32.2	209
	Lib/SDP	7,780,949	25.4	3.5	23
	Con	13,760,583	42.3	57.8	376
1987	Lab	10,029,807	30.8	35.2	229
	All.	7,341,633	22.5	3.4	22
	Con	14,093,890	41.9	51.6	336
1992	Lab	11,559,734	34.4	41.6	271
	Lib Dem	5,998,378	17.8	3.1	20
	Con	9,600,940	30.7	25.0	165
1997	Lab	13,517,911	43.2	63.4	418
	Lib Dem	5,243,440	16.8	7.0	46

a Women MPs from other parties.

Table compiled with Nigel Currie from *Craig* and *Times Guides to House of Commons*.

Total	Women MPs	Type of government	Labour leader
635	8	Con	Michael Foot
	11	majority 43	(1980)
	0		
650	13	Con	Neil Kinnock
	10	majority 144	(Oct 1983)
	0		
650	17	Con	
	21	majority 102	
	2+1[a]		
651	20	Con	John Smith
	37	majority 21	(July 1992)
	2+1[a]		Tony Blair
			(July 1994)
659	13	Lab	
	101	majority 178	
	3+3[a]		

INDEX